ADVENTURES IN ADULTING

A collection of tales, trails, and crucial conversations

TREY GUINN

All artwork created with love by
SHANNON GUINN

Trey Guinn

1.11.20

The author may be reached at: treyguinn.com/adulting

ISBN: 9781081046668

GRATITUDE & DEDICATION

This book and so much else would be impossible without the love and support of Shannon Rose, my wife and hiking buddy for life. We live in constant hope that God grow our hearts to be more like His and that we be used for His glory. We dedicate this book to our children and to everyone who has helped us along the path into and around Adulting Mountain.

DISCLAIMER & REQUESTS

No book will be all things to all people. As case in point, some dismiss or even ridicule what others deem as sacred text and holy scripture. And like anyone, authors carry their own biases and other imperfections. Some of them known; even worse, some unknown. I write painfully aware that I am a flawed human writing an imperfect book. Reader beware! That said, do me this one favor. Give the book a chance. Read with an open mind that perhaps I have things to share with you. In return, I invite you to contact me directly with any feedback, and I will receive it with an open mind, knowing that you may have things to share with me. I'd love to see your stories and feedback in the next iteration of this living document that I call a book. One way to do so is by sharing your crucial conversation reflections online using the links provided.

For now, happy reading.

CONTENTS

CHAPTER 1

ABOUT ADULTING MOUNTAIN

"You already know though. You only live once, that's the motto…YOLO!"

- *Aubrey Drake Graham*

"Keep on moving. Keep climbing. Keep the faith…it's all about… the climb."

- *Miley Cyrus*

Don't be too surprised by the introductory quotes. Funny as it may seem, I have successfully stirred many a classroom debate over the lyrics here and from similar hits.

If good teaching requires that educators meet students where they are, then there is no doubt that pop culture is a great port of entry for educating traditional college students. As a university professor, I've witnessed the most quiet and reserved students passionately debate peers about the meaning of hip-hop lyrics, country tunes, scenes from blockbuster hits, and more.

Perhaps no debates are as memorable as the ones stirred when students go back and forth about the meaning of YOLO—you only live once. As you may recall, YOLO was originally declared to be Drake's motto in the once overplayed hip-hop duet with Lil Wayne.

Most students quickly come to a consensus that the meaning of YOLO is a bit devilish by arguing that it means, "Hey, life is short. There are no real consequences. Be selfish and have all the fun you can." On occasion, however, some in class vehemently contest that, even while the song celebrates the party lifestyle typical to hip-hop music, Drake is actually appealing to our better angels. The argument seems to be that the lifestyle of luxury and debauchery hyped in the song is made possible only by a YOLO drive and work-ethic.

Now, as you may have realized, *the song is not the point.* For me, such lyrics are just a tool to stimulate dialogue and help people talk about more important stuff. The discussion facilitator in me wants to merely ask questions, listen, and do my part to provoke more dialogue.

I believe the YOLO debate brings to light some interesting and diverging perspectives on what it really means to live life to the fullest.

What does YOLO mean to you?

Forget about the song and the singer. For a moment, just focus on the motto – You Only Live Once. In class, the varying interpretations tend to form a divide between two camps.

There are those who see YOLO as something like a permission to party (e.g., death is next, so live it up, buy that stuff you want, and party hard now because you only live once and tomorrow is no guarantee) versus those who hear the song as a motivation to grind (e.g., you only live once so hustle hard, take no sick days, grind and strive to be a best version of yourself).

Adulting is a lot like hiking

Let's imagine for a moment that the YOLO motto really is a call to wake each day hyper-motivated to give the day our best, grind hard, and go extreme. In that case, each morning may feel like a new opportunity to either kick it at the campsite or throw on the boots and get hiking. I am going to suspect that you are not a basecamper who sticks at the bottom of the mountain while others hike about. Instead, I picture that you are made for Adulting Mountain, someone likely to embrace the YOLO motivation to live your best and fullest life today, tomorrow, and every day.

Inspired by our newfound meaning of YOLO, imagine we all tie our laces, snap on our packs, and move toward the trailhead. BUT, not so fast. Before we can take a single step on the path, our friend Miley Cyrus comes in like a wrecking ball and decides to offer her two cents.

She leans over and whispers to you that the point of hiking is not about summitting the top of the mountain. Instead, Miley reminds you, it's about the climb.

And what if she is right? Most might agree that life at basecamp sounds pretty basic, but what is so wrong with keeping your eyes on the mountaintops while hiking?

It's all about... the climb

I turned 37 the other day. I've now legally been an adult for more than half of my life. Put another way, I've been an adult for longer than it takes to be considered one.

The thing I am learning about *adulting* is that Miley is right—there is no aha or actual arrival. It is the climb. There are plenty of lookout points and even seasons for pitching a tent and setting up camp for a while, but no endgame.

By comparison, adulting is really unique from other seasons of life. I don't recall being an infant or toddler. I blocked most of middle school from memory, and I can't opine about the golden ages as I've not yet arrived. But I can tell you that when it comes to those adulting years—when you are old enough to vote and fight in a war but too young for social security or senior discounts at hotels and restaurants—there is no shortcut to the summit and no real exit from the mountain. It's a climb. All of it.

The more I read, learn from others, and experience adulting myself, the more I come to believe that a secret to doing it well is to find joy, meaning, and contentment in the grind; the everyday hiking and climbing.

If I am right, let's imagine a world where YOLO is not about indulgence and partying but rather is a motto for waking each day inspired to be your best self—to hike well. And in this world, being your best self and hiking well is not measured by who reaches mountain tops first, grabs the biggest finisher medals, and snaps the best celebration selfies.

Instead, the point of all that hiking has nothing to do with arriving, but just hiking well. Period. In that case, the climb would be both the purpose and the goal. And a full life would not be about parties at basecamp or selfies on the summit. We would focus on *The Climb* because *YOLO*.

...

Waking up at basecamp

Turning 18 and graduating from high school tends to happen around the same time. Emerging adults take some final exams, cap-and-gown-it, and then begin a season of holding—that gap of a few days, weeks, perhaps a summer, or for some even longer—before beginning to do whatever they opt to do next.

Many people I know can identify a clear line dividing their life before high school graduation and their life after. And I think that is because of what seems to be a societal view that young people fall under a cozy umbrella of childhood. This umbrella serves as a shield for a good many young people facing life's challenges—up through high school graduation that is.

Under the umbrella of childhood many find that they can make a mistake or two with minimal consequence, do things just for fun without someone claiming they are squandering time, and even sleep-in on occasion without much judgment. Then graduation happens, and many must kiss the umbrella of childhood goodbye.

Without the umbrella, young people encounter the grand inquisition where everyone—neighbors, relatives, and passerby alike—asks with an eyebrow raised a variety of questions which all sound something like, "So, what are you going to do with your life now?"

Yes, to take off the graduation cap is to walk out from under the umbrella of childhood. Said another way: to graduate high school and experience all the feels of being an adult—some chosen and others imposed—is like you have just woken up at basecamp; the bottom of your new mountain.

You wake to the sun rising on a new day, and you recognize limitless options before you. The first choice, of course, is whether you will actually lace your boots and hike. You see, at basecamp there are many others. Naturally, there are new hikers like you. There are also those that seem to have parked it there for an indefinite period of time, perhaps to avoid the trails for now at least. These individuals are the basecampers.

Awake, alert, and deciding what to do next, you can't help but hear, both audibly and from within, the perennial question, "Where are you headed?" Facing the hike ahead, some deny the new reality, some attempt to defer the responsibility, and others lace their boots and hike.

Basecampers

Sadly, at the foot of Adulting Mountain, there are many reality deniers and responsibility escape artists (i.e., "basecampers"). Though they may look like hikers and dress the part, they tend to stick around basecamp and don't dare venture far.

I've known many individuals who qualify as adults who refrain from adulting. They may even enroll in college courses. Some even hold a job. But when it's time to do the real adulting, they avoid all eye contact and look down at their phone as though they were receiving an important call.

To the basecamper, the reality of adulting is no good and to be avoided at all costs. With a gaming console or Netflix remote in one hand, they huff about how annoyed they are about that thing due tomorrow. Scared to face the elements, they desperately try to stay under the umbrella of childhood. Without a parent or caregiver hovering and helping, the car would never get an oil change and that doctor's appointment would never be made. When problems arise or a deadline is missed, it is always the fault and responsibility of someone else ("I didn't know I was supposed to... but you didn't remind me.").

Like money for nothing and things for free, everyone wants the great views that come with hiking, but fewer are willing to hike to get there. Yet for an adult to ever experience the fullness and freedom of adulting, they must equally embrace the responsibilities. The problem is that the comforts of childhood appear too good for some to grow out of and move on from.

The reality, of course, is that with the comforts of childhood come its confines. No more should an adult cling to childhood comforts than an adolescent sleep in their toddler bed. In the metamorphosis of life, adults should hike as butterflies shall fly. You hardly see a butterfly cling to the cocoon or go back to pushing dirt. Thus, we ought not see an adult cling to basecamp or go back to being coddled under the umbrella of childhood. Adulting muscles are growing with every step of hiking and acceptance of responsibility. Hikers may stumble or venture the wrong way but still be gaining the muscles needed for the path that lies ahead.

This is not to suggest that one must hike alone. Wisdom, support, great coaching and cheering from parents, mentors, loved ones, and close friends is a treasured gift to any hiker.

When mom calls to remind that it's time for your annual check-up don't leave it as her responsibility. Rather, thank her for the reminder and assure her that you will be more than happy to schedule it yourself.

There is no excuse of being too busy. In life, we make time for the things that matter. And for everything else we make excuses.

Being responsible for yourself and your own affairs, like due dates, bills, and appointments, is a top priority as you enter the trail of adulting. It is a small step but important leap out of basecamp and onto the mountain.

When emerging adults don't take those small steps out of basecamp—assuming small yet important responsibilities for themselves—their necessary hiking muscles will not grow; worse, they may atrophy. I've known many nice people who can hold a job and manage happy hour conversation, but they do little, if any, actual adulting.

Time goes by and they grow resentful or jealous as their peers grow hiking muscles and begin to blaze trails along the mountainside.

These individuals often lose their will to hike, if ever they had one, because of a false belief that adulting is too hard—meaning bad. And since it is bad, it must be avoided. Similar false beliefs are held about other important things like having a healthy diet and keeping an exercise routine. It's like the myth that there are math people and non-math people. The reality is that "math people" are those who do the math problems, ask for help as needed, and take the time necessary to figure them out. "Non-math" people are those that stopped doing the math problems because they got hard. This faulty reasoning—it looks hard, which equals bad, and should therefore be avoided—sadly extends to perceptions of adulting.

Faux adulting is relegating oneself to a life at basecamp. In comparison to actual hiking, basecamp—by its proximity to the mountain—provides the illusion of adulting and many of the comforts and amenities of childhood, but without the actual hiking! And there is way less (if any) sweating! Tempting perhaps, but basecamp is the fool's gold of Adulting Mountain. It's a thing, but not the real thing.

Many young adults I know claim to be adulting because their driver's license says they are one. But a close look at their responsibility-avoidant lifestyle betrays them.

Ironically, basecampers speak poetically about summitting and have vivid social media plans for once they reach the top, yet they haven't stepped one foot onto the trail. Meanwhile, those actually adulting enter the mountain, hit the trail, get sweaty, and reap the benefits of *becoming*. They grow, develop, and are refined by the new experiences and incredible interactions they have along the way.

Sadly still, adulting-avoiders keep the fire warm at basecamp and build Pinterest boards full of what their mansion on the summit will look like. The tragically trapped mind of the basecamper dreams of the summit while camped at the base; nothing but false comfort and misplaced hope.

Distracted Hiking

While basecamp is full of reality deniers and responsibility escape artists, the mountain itself is also full of distracted hikers. Like distracted *drivers*, these individuals do the hiking, but are doing so focused on all the wrong things. For varying reasons, each of them seems to have missed Miley's memo—it's the climb.

Some of them hike with a huff and in a hurry. They could be considered the aggressive drivers of the mountain as they move with their eyes glued to the clock or the paces and paths of other hikers. Either way, they are consumed with getting around and getting ahead. Their efforts appear exhausting and are in vain because—just like aggressive drivers—they appear to get nowhere fast enough and then sulk when they realize everyone wound up at about the same spot around the same time.

Other types of distracted drivers may be less concerned with getting around you because they are more concerned with trying to be you, be like you, be better than you, or simply be liked by you. At any rate, they have no time to enjoy their hike because the object of their attention is you, the path you are on, and perhaps even your hiking gear of choice. They are consumed with comparing themselves to you and everyone else. If they could they would share their hike on their story or feed, and then rather than look out and enjoy the trail, they would just stare at their device and wait to see if *you* "liked" their trail.

Another type of distracted hiker is completely oblivious to you, the path, or anything really. The focus of their thoughts and object of their eyes is reaching the summit.

And then that summit. Oh, shoot, and then the next one. Their laser-beam focus on only the mountaintops is distracting them from the present here and now and causes them to trip over themselves, bump into fellow hikers, and inadvertently stomp over the roses that others are stopping to smell. Some learn to leverage others to summit faster, but, even then, their eyes remain focused on the next mountaintop. There are many admirable things to be said about their commitment and fervor, and many of them accomplish so much and reach incredible heights. But with all that stock placed on the next mountaintop moment, the actual thrill of summitting is gone the moment they see a higher peak to reach. Sadly, many may wake to realize they are atop a mountain without anyone to share it and with few memories actually made.

The distracted hikers have misplaced and unbalanced focus. Some are too heavily focused on beating, being like, or being liked by all the hikers around them. Others hike with eyes locked on reaching summits that never quite fulfill. Whatever the reason for the distracted hiking, it's clear these individuals are living unaware or perhaps in denial that *it's the climb*. While they move their feet all along the mountain, they seem to miss the hike altogether and often fail to notice until regrettably too late.

Hang-ups, hardships, and hangovers

All hikers encounter challenges on the mountain. There are blisters, storms, loss, and getting lost, just to name a few. And most hikers can learn to manage a set-back or hang-up here and there, but when they pile on it can become unbearable for some.

Hiking through rain and sheltering a storm is one thing, but waking to blisters and missing gear may be enough to make the happiest camper scream. Similarly, I've known plenty of friends to lose their job or get dumped by the person they loved. Both in the same week, however, may feel like cruel and unusual torture. Some hardships and emotional hurts, especially when piled on, can appear to be insurmountable impediments and become a psychological block for many hikers.

Even healthy hikers may allow for hang-ups or hardships to become cause for unhealthy habits, poor choices, or even next-day hangovers. I've witnessed wonderful people succumb to slothfulness, turn to substances, or in some cases both. And I've known great people to take sad and lengthy detours through dark valleys or even make complete turnarounds to basecamp.

I actually encountered a bit of this myself during a particularly painful and challenging season. Determined to hike ahead, I refused to stop for help, and developed habits of fueling with coffee and keeping my spirit lifted with spirits. I thought I could heal myself and hike ahead. But I needed real help, like a healing touch from Heaven and good community to coach and cheer me back into healthy hiking. I thank God for sending good people into my life who helped me learn better ways for hiking onward!

To one extent or another, hang-ups, hardships, and hangovers are part of adulting. They can strike you unexpectedly and may expose parts of you—like how you *really* respond to life. While we may not always be able to control what happens to us, I believe we can (almost) always control how we respond. Similarly, we can't choose the weather and might get hit unexpected with a storm, BUT we can choose how to hike through it. Many can remain pleasant on a sunny day, but how you behave through a storm speaks volumes.

When you get knocked down hard, will you crawl to the corner and cope through it? Or will you do the humbling work of asking for the help and healing needed to hike again?

The mountain is for adults committed to responsible hiking. This requires that one avoid distracted hiking and seek true healing from hardships, hurts and hang-ups. Anything less is to render yourself unfit to hike and a hazard to those who are.

Hiking Buddies

Perhaps one of the best parts of hiking is all the incredible people you can meet on the mountain. As you begin to hike, you discover that other hikers have different objectives and approaches from you. Some want to hike fast and far, while others want to take it slow and steady. And some may appear naïve and underprepared, while others appear to be intensely focused and perhaps overprepared.

Your hike will have peaks. Inevitably, valleys too. There will be surprises—some welcome, others not. The techniques you learn from others will prove invaluable when you face something you least expected. This is why you must make time to listen and learn from other hikers.

Listening to and learning from others is a way to show love as well as develop and grow as a hiker. I have found most people are honored by those who care enough to listen. And I have discovered I grow tremendously from their stories—hearing how she made it through that one tough patch inspires me, and learning how he found the inner-strength to endure the downpour and hike anyway, serves as an incredible testimony to me. Compassionately love and eagerly learn from the basecampers and distracted hikers too. Even if someone hikes differently than you, hearing their story and learning from them grows your empathy and appreciation for others. It also helps you to discover and refine your own objectives and approaches to life on the mountain.

Adulting mountain is a wonderful place to discover friendships and partnerships that may last a season or a lifetime. And because friendship can be a perfect place for romantic love to bloom, where better to find that special hiking buddy than on a hike through Adulting Mountain?

There are seasons when you and your hiking partner(s) may choose to set up camp, get comfortable and settle in for a bit. And to clarify, setting camp on the mountain and delighting in the journey is not at all the same as making home at basecamp. One is to find special ways to celebrate the joy of hiking, the other is to avoid hiking altogether.

Adulting Mountain offers unexpectedly breathtaking views. There is indescribable pain of walking on blisters. There are days you plan for sunshine but get caught in a rainstorm. You get lost down a path you were sure was right. You explore the unknown and find yourself all over again.

Best of all, you meet hiking buddies along the way. You capture a heart and hope to never have yours broken. You trade stories that make you laugh and cry. You share secrets and make new ones.

All this and more can be found on Adulting Mountain where we don't passively let life happen to us. Instead, we purposefully pursue trails, create and share meaningful tales, and have crucial conversations about who we are becoming. We get serious about the kind of people we are, the way we relate with others, and the work we do.

So, lace your boots. You were made for hiking. The journey will be spectacular.

CRUCIAL
CONVERSATIONS

What about you—are you feeling inspired to hike?

What are some additional ways that you believe adulting is like hiking?

What have been your experiences with basecamp? Or perhaps distracted hiking? Or have you known people to struggle with either?

Why are these such easy traps to fall into? And how can people avoid them?

How have you seen hang-ups, hardships, or hangovers hinder otherwise healthy and happy hikers?

What are the qualities you hope for most in your hiking buddies? What qualities do you bring to future hiking buddies? In other words, why might someone want to be your hiking buddy?

......

Want to share this conversation with Trey, or perhaps even see your thoughts in a future version of this book?

Go to treyguinn.com/adulting and share!

CHAPTER 2

WHO WILL YOU BECOME?

This book is a sharing of stories strung together to help readers wrestle with some big proclamations that I pose as being relevant for those embarking upon and reflecting on the journey through adulting: you are worthy, you are the content of your character, and more.

I suspect that the stories and claims here may cause laughter, raise eyebrows, and possibly invite disagreement. Most of all, I hope this book invites critical reflection, as well as encourages you to wrestle with big ideas and ask worthy questions.

One of the realities of adulting is that we raise more questions than we answer, and not all questions should be weighted equally.

Such is the case with the familiar question—*what will you become?*—that we regularly ask young people and those embarking on adulthood. The question is not altogether a bad one, but it misplaces priority from what I believe are more important questions for young people to answer.

Who will you become?

The room was filled primarily with recent high school graduates, their parents and siblings, and I suppose any others that had been roped into attending. I had just completed my prepared remarks during summer orientation for incoming college students. I left the stage and walked into the audience to ask for any questions. The first couple questions were softballs and fun to answer. Then a well-meaning but stern dad stood up, adjusted his pants by the belt (always a sign that a tough question is coming), and said, "This is all good stuff to know, but when he's done and graduates from this program, what do we expect he will actually become?"

To be clear, this is a fair question. College is expensive, and people want to know the actual ROI—return on investment. This dad, like many others, had a practical concern: this is a lot of money, so what will we get in return?

Put another way: if my kid comes here and studies with you, *what will he become*? When that is the first question you get, you can almost guarantee that the next one will be something like, "And how *much* does that job pay?"

This line of questioning exposes how the argument for higher education can quickly boil down to input versus output. Or money in versus money out. If we invest this much into a degree, what will we become and how much will we earn with said degree? I wish this weren't the case. But I understand how we got here.

For starters, the cost of higher education has and continues to increase painfully so. Have you been on a college tour recently? A good many that I've witnessed go something like this: "Welcome. Enjoy a latte at the football stadium. Next, take a try at our climbing wall, and then enjoy a refreshing smoothie from our rec center. After that we can try some fresh quesadillas out by the lazy river. Oh, and if you want, you can sit in on a class tomorrow."

Forgive me for the slight exaggeration. But the exaggeration is only slight. If college tours sound like competing country club memberships, then why should universities expect students to act like anything less than club members who see their bill each month and (re)weigh the costs against the perks of membership? As the price hikes higher, you can expect people to critique the product more and more.

In San Antonio, where I am from, imagine what would happen if you saw a disproportionate escalation in the price of breakfast tacos. If the same breakfast taco cost $2 when my oldest daughter ate it, but now costs $4 for her little sister, you best believe I want to know what accounts for the price hike?

Gawking at the inflated price, I'm now determined to learn just what the heck comes with that breakfast taco? Is the $4 one twice as big or twice as good? And how do you quantify that? Size of taco? Ingredients used? Homemade tortilla versus store bought? This is kind of how we treat college costs. We've always expected a return on investment, but thanks to inflating prices, we demand it.

So, it should be no surprise that people increasingly look at the price tag of college and say things like, "Ok, given what this cost, just what exactly will I become when I get out of here? And how much does that make?" This is just one cause for people to obsess over career attainment. There is also undue societal pressure on what people (should) become. I place parenthesis around the word should because there are at least two phases where people face the pressure and evaluation over what they become.

First, when you are young, presumably capable of becoming anything, there is the season of life when individuals overtly or covertly wield influence over what you *should* become even from statements like, "Oh honey, you don't want to become an X. That is for girls like your sister. You should study Y and become a Z. Plus, it's the only way you will be able to pay back all those student loans."

Second, after it's presumably too late to influence what you *will* become, there is that phase of life when you have or should have already become something. It's that point when people evaluate your worth and value according to what it is that you actually became from statements like, "Oh, you are an X? Well, that is good for you. And we certainly need more people willing to do that kind of work."

Now, don't think your friends with highly regarded careers are off the hook completely. I can't even count the times I have heard a medical doctor or lawyer be criticized for their area of medicine or law not being prestigious enough. Bringing it close to home, a PhD being looked down upon because of where they teach or publish, or even worse, if they left higher education and took a job in industry. Judging others according to *what* they (should) become is a sad and pathetic social pastime.

Who are you becoming?

No matter my audience or venue—university classroom, conference center, business leaders, or you-name-it—I really want people to pause, take inventory of their life, and think about something else; a higher-order question. Eliminate the noise that surrounds *WHAT you will become* and get serious about *WHO you are becoming.*

At the orientation when that dad asked me the question, I began with a generic response to satisfy his curiosity about potential careers and job market, but I also transitioned my answer toward what I care deeply about—that people everywhere pay close attention to WHO they are becoming.

Yes, WHAT you will become—a job or some other title—matters, but nowadays, professional pathways shift with emerging technologies, and people change their career like they change apartments, vehicles, and service providers. Alternatively, and especially during the season of adulting, WHO you will become is so much more important to me.

As a university professor, I have found that college is a special environment ripe for wrestling with big questions like these, just as a long road-trip with your family or friends, a retreat with your church group, or professional development with your colleagues. I hope you wrestle with the big questions everywhere you go both independently and collectively with the people you choose to do life with.

I applaud you now for the efforts you will make toward discovering and shaping the person that you are becoming. Who you are becoming is the real you—the inside that wants out. That's part of what adulting is about. It's about doing the heavy lifting to discover a deeper, richer, more meaningful understanding of self, and taking responsibility for all you are and all you are becoming.

This book is my invitation to dialogue together as you embark and/or reflect upon your own journey through adulting. Many of the stories shared here are ones I tell my college students, as well as learners across the globe. My stories are not profound. My insights are not scriptural truth. Rather, they are simply my stories and insights. My goal is not to have you agree with my answers, but that you intentionally and thoughtfully wrestle with big questions. I am sharing a few of my trails and tales in hopes of it inspiring you to reflect a bit, and perhaps engage, in some crucial conversations about who you are becoming.

Name it and claim it

When I was about 20 years old, finishing college, and looking forward to graduate school, I was invited to help my university revamp our programs for incoming students. Part of that programming included that all incoming students would take a strengths assessment. Don't think anything like push-up or bench-press competitions. Instead, a strengths-finder assessment is a way to help pinpoint five ways a person is naturally gifted, talented, and thrives.

Examples would be having the strength of *competition* or *positivity*. You can certainly imagine someone you know who is hard-wired to turn all things into a competition (even a flight of stairs becomes "race you to the top"), and these individuals seem to derive a unique level of motivation and purpose when competing. Likewise, you can certainly imagine someone you know who sees the positive side of everything all the time (flat tire on their way to an important meeting and they proclaim, "It's my lucky day—I have a spare in the trunk!").

More than fifteen years later, and I still get to help groups discover their strengths. Earlier this year I worked with a group of NCAA championship athletes and coaches. Guess how many of them had competition in their top five strengths?

When working with groups, it is not uncommon for someone to complete the questionnaire and seminar all to conclude that they felt the assessment failed to capture the truth about who they are and which strengths they identified with best. For example, someone will say to me, "I think I am an *activator*, but the test doesn't say so," to which I reply, "Name it and claim it. If you believe you are an activator, then I do too! Let's write it on your sheet."

That is what I have done in this book. I have taken a few things that I value and hope to be true for my life, and I have named them and claimed them. I invite you to do the same.

CRUCIAL CONVERSATIONS

What about you—have you been asked repeatedly about what you are going to do with your life and *what* you will become?

Why do you think people commonly evaluate others based on what they (should) become?

Why might "_who_ will you become?" be a more important, albeit harder, question to answer than "what will you become?"

What are some things that you might want to name and claim to be true for your life? And why is that?

......

Want to share this conversation with Trey, or perhaps even see your thoughts in a future version of this book?

Go to treyguinn.com/adulting and share!

PART 1

WHO YOU ARE

I was talking with a student the other day, and he began to debate me about the nature of impression management. He was griping that it's not fair that people judge you based on the way you dress, walk, talk, etc. As I listened more, I realized the crux of his argument came down to, "why should I have to change who I am and dress up for a job interview? This is me. I gotta be me." He brought up an important point—one that I have heard before and expect to hear again. I explained to him that adulting is often about ordering and prioritizing multiple goals. Dress how I feel and say what I want aren't bad goals; they just pale in comparison to bigger goals like winning a job interview, especially if things like paying your phone bill and eating this month are important to you.

The whole "I gotta be/do me" attitude, I believe, can often come down to ego and pride or perhaps an unfortunate misunderstanding of how to think about and prioritize adult goals.

If I was hellbent on "doing me," then I would show up to my office in running shorts every day. I'd play my music loudly and skip meetings in order to grab more midday runs. But in that case, I would not have a job for long. So, you know what? I decided a long time ago that "doing me" is not my first goal. Or, put another way, the first order of business in "doing me" is about accomplishing big goals, and, to accomplish big goals, at times I need to amend my default behaviors. For most people, the me we got to be is employed. If ironing a shirt and shaving increases the chance of getting hired, grab the iron and razor. Let's do this!

There are some who may still push back and say something like, "But that's you not being your real self." If so, I politely urge you to consider the nature of your disagreement. What is being threatened here? Some might say they are protecting authentic self. Fair point. I'd argue that those willing to amend their behavior are protecting authentic self too.

For me, being me and my true self is to be someone who accomplishes exciting goals. And, if with a good conscience, I can adapt my behavior—dressing up or dressing down, less humor or more humor, smiling through a conversation even when I am dead tired—one way or another in order to accomplish my goals more effectively, then I am being very true to myself.

...

My family and I were on vacation a couple weekends ago. While lounging by the lazy river with a book in hand, the nice people brought our food out. At the exact moment when I went to set down my book and begin to eat, a bee decided to land on my nose. It stayed there for over five minutes. For those five minutes, I sat perfectly still and did not talk or move, much less touch my food.

My wife, our kids, and people nearby could hardly hold back their laughter and commentary. Rather than "do me" and behave naturally as intended, I amended everything about my behavior to prevent being stung.

The bee was tiny in comparison to me. I was hungry and wanted to eat with my family. But more importantly, I did not want to get stung. If something so small and insignificant as one little bee could put such a monkey wrench in my natural way of being, then why on earth would I dismiss good advice on how to best adapt my behavior for something important like winning the favor of my professor with a polite email or gaining favor from my boss by showing extra courtesy and respect?

Amending behaviors, adapting to others and your environment, and developing as a person does not pose a threat to "doing me" any more than lifting weights poses a threat to the status of my body before entering the gym. Let "doing me" be about growing into a person who accomplishes big goals set by you, even if that requires evolving in terms of how you do you. Yes, I got to be me, BUT I also get to choose the me I be.

Adulting is not just about looking in the mirror and declaring what you see; it is about asking what you wish to see and who you aspire to be in days to come. Each tale I tell and trail I've traversed says a bit about who I've been and who I am, but the most crucial part is who I am becoming.

Don't just tell me who you are. Tell me who you are becoming. Name it and claim it!

CRUCIAL CONVERSATIONS

What about you—do you ever wrestle with the "I gotta do me" attitude? Can you imagine ways that this thinking is a bit of a double-edged sword? —helpful on occasion, but otherwise a hinderance?

Sometimes adulting requires ordering your goals. What goals of yours are bigger than the goal of "doing me"?

......

Want to share this conversation with Trey, or perhaps even see your thoughts in a future version of this book?

Go to treyguinn.com/adulting and share!

CHAPTER 3

YOU ARE WORTHY

"There are no ifs, ands, or buts about it.

You are worthy. You were born worthy.

You will die worthy. Nothing can change that."

-     *Me speaking to you*

"Wait! We forgot to do the worthy pledge!" James, a smaller than average fifth-grader shouts it one more time, "Ma'am, we forgot the worthy pledge!" Hoping to be heard over the competing voices of his classmates, he skips to get in front of her face and waits for their eyes to lock.

He is determined to be heard, and rightfully so. The worthy pledge is serious business for this classroom of fifth graders. To them, the worthy pledge is sacrosanct like the pledge of allegiance, snack-time, and recess.

From the first day of the academic year until schools-out-for-summer, these fifth graders rise daily to perform the worthy pledge. They know the drill and do it to perfection with as much fervor as a high school marching band under Friday night lights.

Go back to fifth grade for a moment. Imagine standing with your peers and doing the following:

(From front of the room, the teacher says)
"Ok, everybody hands on your heart. Ready?"

(Each student, with hand over heart, proudly proclaims)
"I am worthy!"

(The teacher says)
"Now turn to your neighbors."

(Each student quickly turns to as many students nearby and says)
"You are worthy! And you are worthy!
And you're worthy! And you too!
All of you are worthy!"

Admittedly, when first hearing the idea, I was not convinced this would take off. I mean, the thought of standing and declaring aloud my own worthiness and then proclaiming yours was hard for me to truly imagine. But earlier this year, that gorgeous fifth-grade teacher (who happens to also be my wife) invited me to visit her class, and I witnessed the worthy pledge in-person. The lift in the classroom was unmistakable.

On the drive home I kept thinking about how fifth graders aren't the only ones who could use a worthy pledge.

…

Just last week, I met with a medical doctor in Austin, Texas. He is a client of mine who originally booked time for help with presentation skills and interpersonal savvy. Within a few sessions of working together, our discussions took a sharp turn toward issues about self-confidence and some longstanding issues with insecurity.

It turns out that my doctor-client feels plenty sure of himself when making the rounds to see patients and talking in the hallways with hospital staff. Confidence oozes out of every pore, he says. That all fades away, however, the moment he enters a room with a higher-ranking doctor, or when his doctor-peers question his decision-making.

Like many of us, there are certain triggers that cause my client to revert to a smaller insecure self. A self who frequently asks, "Am I worthy?" A self that craves some identifiable indication that someone, usually a specific someone(s), accepts who we are, approves of what we have done, and deems us worthy. And this craving wreaks havoc on my client by causing him to lose focus, and to wrestle with thoughts, feelings, and beliefs about himself that are negative, hurtful, and disabling.

The trouble does not stop there for the good doctor. I learned that his question of worthiness is like a nagging "what does *that* person think of me *right now?*" High praise from colleagues on a Monday morning don't sustain him for the day, much less the week.

In fact, I know he shows up to work most days with flooding thoughts about whether he is worthy to wear the white coat. And it is not just work. His fiancé might text kissy faces and hearts throughout the day, but after work when they meet for dinner he is preoccupied with thoughts of whether she still loves him and wants to be with him. He thinks his parents are proud that he is a doctor, but each trip home during the holidays brings about uneasy feelings about what his dad will think of him *now*.

My doctor client is a great example of wrestling with worth, because here you have a very bright person who has accomplished what so many others dream to accomplish. He is a bonafide medical doctor. I've known and taught countless college students who act as though their livelihood and value depends on becoming a doctor, a lawyer, or some other vocation that society deems worthy. Yet I have numerous doctors, lawyers, pro-athletes, and c-suite executives for clients who reach their vocational dreams only to realize that their confidence, inner-security, and self-worth remain unstable still. But why?

...

"Ya, we like Katie, she's really cool."

"Ugh. Katie's lame."

"Wow! Katie, you run so fast!"

"Wow. Katie, you are so slow."

"Hey, we want Katie in our group!"

"No, we don't want her. You all take Katie in your group."

The utterances of others who we allow to fuel or siphon our self-worth may sound different across a number of variables such as age, gender, etc. Re-read the statements a few lines up, just the ones on the left side of the page, but interchange your name and a descriptor or two, and then imagine the person(s) you would want to hear it from most. Oh, how sweet the sound!

Conversely, travel back to a time you heard something like those statements on the right side. Ugh, the agony.

It does not matter how old you are. Just like my doctor client, inside of you and me is a longing to feel worthy and accepted as we are without conditions. Here is the good news: you don't need to wait until you have your dream relationship to feel worthy. You don't need to make the dean's list to feel worthy. You don't need to achieve each of your professional goals to be deemed worthy.

Those 5th graders are right! YOU ARE WORTHY!
So, once and for all, declare it: I AM WORTHY!

There are no ifs, ands, or buts about it. You are worthy. You were born worthy. You will die worthy. There is nothing that can change that.

You can ace every exam from here until eternity, or you can sleep through your next exam (although I highly advise against it). Your worth, however, remains unchanged.

If you believe me that you are worthy, if you can accept that this reality is unchanging, and if you want to seal that deal and make the worthy pledge, then I want you to take this next step.

Imagine that you can take your self-worth and set it in a treasure chest—much like you would a precious heirloom.

With your self-worth placed safely inside the treasure chest, close and lock it with a key. Now, here is the important part—what to do with the key? The integrity of your self-worth is now only as safe as that key. So, who should hold that key?

The mistake that most people make is they walk around the world with their key out for any taker.

- *Mr. popular guy at school, here is the key to my self-worth. What do you think? Am I worthy?*
- *Hey Dad, I made honor-roll. NBD, really, but just curious... What do you think? Am I worthy yet?*
- *Beep. Beep. Not sure if you all noticed my new ride. (Not sure I can afford the payments, but surely my confidence meter can get some mileage from this thing.)*
- *Hey cute person at work, any chance you have noticed me yet? I mean, here is the key to my self-worth... So, whatcha think? Am I worthy?*
- *Oh, excuse me, important person in my social circle, here is the key to my self-worth. What do you think? Am I invited to the summer social? If not, that's cool. I'll just retreat to my world of unworthiness and scope all the fun on your Instagram account, dreaming of what it might be like to someday be worthy enough.*

The examples above are silly enough to feel exaggerated, yet simple enough to make the point. It does not matter the age, gender, or whatever particular nuance about the person I am working with, examples like the ones above always strike a chord.

It seems that somewhere in us we are wired to determine what others think of us. And the root of what we want to know is, "Am I accepted? And, am I worthy?"

So, knowingly or unknowingly, we may allow *our perceptions of* others' opinion of us to shape our self-worth. Notice that italicized phrase in the sentence above. There are times we might actually know others' opinions of us, but mostly we are working off what we perceive.

I can recall a number of three-way calling in high school that went horribly wrong. "Trey, I am going to call you and then secretly call her on three way. I'll talk to her and then slyly ask what she thinks of you, and then you will know exactly what she thinks." Brilliant plan, so I thought. Within moments it was quite clear.

"Oh, Trey? I mean, why are we even talking about him? Sure, he's nice and kind of sweet in like a little brother way, I guess... But... I mean, no, just no. Not cute at all."

So, there is that. Sometimes we might actually <u>know</u> a person's opinion of us, or at least the opinion they share with others when not knowing that we are listening. It should go without mentioning that the secret three-way calling that so many of us did in the day of landline phones was just really dumb. Major lapse in judgment. Be better than that!

However, most of the time we operate from merely *our perceptions* of others' opinions of us. We don't *actually* know the inner thoughts of others, much less whether they *actually* think about us and, if so, what those thoughts of us might be. Yet, a good many of us are convinced that others do have thoughts about us, and we assume to know what those thoughts about us are.

Even still, imagine that somehow, on the wild and rare occasion, you got all of that right — that someone did have thoughts about you and you accurately perceived them— what impact should that have on your actual self-worth? Why should that person(s) be trusted with the key to your treasure chest marked "Self-Worth"?

CRUCIAL CONVERSATIONS

And what about you—how often do you wrestle with the questions about "am I accepted?" or "am I worthy?"

How do questions like this shape your thoughts, attitudes, beliefs about yourself… or perhaps even your behavior?

What about your self-worth treasure chest? How many keys have been made and distributed? Who do you allow to hold keys and why?

If you believed that your self-worth was a precious gem, to be protected at all cost, what would you do to reclaim the misplaced keys securing it?

......

Want to share this conversation with Trey, or perhaps even see your thoughts in a future version of this book?

Go to treyguinn.com/adulting and share!

Another predator preys on our self-worth

We have established that cravings for acceptance, approval, and perceptions of others' opinions can severely compromise self-worth. Here, we should recognize that there are other enemies of self-worth that merit mentioning: guilt and shame.

One thing that breaks my heart is witnessing people with enormous potential for bright and beautiful futures stand under dark clouds of guilt and shame.

As a product of my vocation, I see this most in traditional-aged college students. I have not left the college scene since first arriving in the fall of 2000, and I hope to never leave. I'd be perfectly happy working at a university forevermore, and a critical reason why is because of the rich conversations I have with students. I learn from them every day, and I do my best to make sure they learn something from me too!

One thing I have learned from college students is that lots of people carry bags everywhere they go. Not just backpacks of overpriced textbooks and all that. I mean terribly heavy bags of junk that wear people down.

Countless times a student will approach me in the classroom, my office, or anywhere in between, to talk about life, something from class, a bit of good news, and frequently some hard stuff too. Sometimes, we get talking about heavier things—like self-worth.

What's usually easy for me to spot, albeit painful to see, is a beautiful soul being weighed down by bags of guilt or shame and all that yucky stuff.

A sad but too common situation is one like Erin's. From across the room and in brief interaction, you would easily assume Erin had a charmed life. She got to college on great grades and a sterling resume. Erin is an attractive person that seems to be always smiling, laughing, and dressed well. I can hardly imagine someone thinking otherwise. She scheduled time to chat during my office hours, and the more she spoke, the quicker I spotted the signs of a hurting soul.

I listened for understanding and prayed for a good and right word to share as she spoke. In full disclosure, I should share here that I am a praying person. I believe that God opens enormous doors for me, and as I walk through them, I am utterly dependent on Him as a lamp unto my feet and a light unto my path as onward I go.

So, whether I am teaching or giving a big presentation, working with clients or meeting with a heavy-hearted person, I am relying on God in that moment to guide my speech and my steps. People always talk about how their success is the product of their preparation. Without question, my greatest preparation is prayer.

There I spoke with Erin. Praying for discernment from God, hoping for divine intervention and some wise words. And, there it came from the heavens... nothing! So, I said.... nothing!

I smiled, listened, and eventually over the course of the first few minutes, uttered things like, "Tell me more about that." God's answer to my prayer seemed to be, "Just listen."

And to no credit of my own, she started talking about life. She shared with me some painful stuff from her past. What struck me though was how she spoke of her past. Sure, she talked about stuff that happened in the past, but it was obvious to me that she was ruminating on it as if it were her present.

Now, you can probably recall times when you spoke to someone retelling a story where there is clear distance from their yesterday and today. And then sometimes people talk about their past and it's like they are still living in it.

A phrase like "reliving the past" may cause you to picture an older guy retelling his glory-day, football stories like it was last night, albeit they happened 40+ years ago. And this would be a humorous and appropriate example of someone living in the past.

But what I am talking about, in this case, is people like Erin. A sophomore in college, she had her whole world ahead of her, yet she couldn't see that. She was waking each day and reliving her past, and this denied her the joy of her present and the promise of her future. Her past pain manifested as her present guilt and shame, and it created a horribly dark cloud over her sense of self-worth.

I eventually reached some clarity about questions to ask. I asked what she saw when she looked in the mirror. She saw a tainted girl, unworthy of good things, incapable of healthy relationships and all that God had for her.

And why, you might ask? Because her self-worth was

being shredded and mauled by daily reliving unwise choices she made in high school. A few regrettable moments with friends and other painful moments with boys she no longer knows yet couldn't seem to forget.

By now, you the reader must certainly know where I am headed here. Tell me: who was holding the key to Erin's self-worth treasure chest? Definitely not her. Nor her parents, loved ones, or God. Not even someone special in her present reality, like a best friend or significant other. Perhaps worst of all, she had relinquished the key to the ghosts of her past. Ghosts like *Shame* and *Guilt*. How tragic!

My heart broke for her as she spoke. At the time, I had just become a new dad, and my own sister was Erin's age; everything paternal and brotherly in me wanted to scream, "You are loved. You are worthy!" I wisely resisted the urge, listened some more, shared a short story about self-worth, took out a piece of paper and drew a key and a treasure chest for her.

...

About a month later she came by the office, pulled an antique looking key out from her purse and dangled it while saying, "There's only one copy, and it's all mine." I nearly cried on cue and asked if she wanted a coffee. She said hopefully soon, but that she had to run to class. It was epic (and I never use that word).

I wish everyone had an antique looking key that guarded the treasure chest of their self-worth. If I had only one copy it would lie in the hands of God.

What would you do with yours?

CRUCIAL
CONVERSATIONS

Really, imagine you could reclaim and burn all copies ever made, and you're left with just one key to your self-worth treasure chest. What would you do with yours?

What are some reasons that people are prone to living in the past? And why are others prone to avoiding their past?

Are you prone to having a past, present, or future orientation? Meaning, where do you tend to focus—on the past, present, or future? And why do you think that is?

Like Erin, are you ever haunted by ghosts like shame and guilt from your past? These villains love to do scary things to our self-worth, but you can choose to revoke their key and render them powerless.

Knowing that you are forever worthy, how can you secure the lock forevermore?

......

Want to share this conversation with Trey, or perhaps even see your thoughts in a future version of this book?

Go to treyguinn.com/adulting and share!

CHAPTER 4

YOU ARE THE CONTENT
OF YOUR CHARACTER

"Intelligence plus character—that is the goal of true education."

- *Martin Luther King, Jr.*

My colleague recently asked me to do a peer-evaluation of his teaching. That's where one teacher asks a fellow teacher to observe them teach and provide them feedback. We do this for fun, and it happens to be a requirement of the job. Or, one might say that it is a requirement of the job that we make fun. I suppose that it's all how you look at it.

Really, I enjoy observing my colleagues teach, and almost always learn something interesting in the process. When my friend asked me to observe his teaching, I asked him to send me any material or pre-readings for the day. That way I would come prepared like any other student in the course. It was a couple of books, so I ordered them in advance and got to reading.

One of the books was David Brooks' Road to Character. The introductory chapter alone could stir enough conversation to last a semester. In it, Brooks introduces the notion of resume virtues versus eulogy virtues.

Oversimplified, Brooks argues that *resume virtues* are those accolades and achievements that tend to impress society and help people secure internships and high-paying jobs, earn prestigious awards and all that stuff. By contrast, *eulogy virtues* are those aspects of character—humility, kindness, bravery, and the like—that we often praise when someone is not around to hear it, like at their funeral. The question or concern that is naturally raised by reading Brooks' book is whether our culture celebrates accumulation of resume virtues at the expense, or to the detriment, of eulogy virtues.

I wondered how much the students would connect with the message, and I also recalled some of my earliest notions of what Brooks might call resume and eulogy virtues. I can remember being a kid and telling my parents that I wanted to be a rich and famous actor, but that I also wanted to give away a lot of my money. Now, hear me out, I do think it's nice when people who have a lot of stuff choose to share it, and it's a good thing when somebody gets older or dies and donates their wealth to those in need. This line of thinking (become wildly successful and then act philanthropically in my older age) I had as a young person, however, is not the same as living in pursuit of eulogy virtues or choosing the road to character.

I now believe we can live responsible lives attuned to resume AND eulogy virtues. So, I argue that we need a generation of leaders mindful of and in pursuit of BOTH.

Students regularly come to my office seeking a recommendation letter or for me to serve as a reference for them in hopes that they get an internship or a summer job. I always inquire a bit about the details and am curious about *why* they want the role they are applying for. I am not surprised when I hear them say that someone told them it would look good for their med-school application, or that they heard it is an easy gig that pays well. And I also don't think less of someone for padding their resume or running an internal cost/benefit analysis.

It would be pretty far-fetched to hear someone say something like they were pursuing an internship because they heard it would advance their eulogy virtues, humble them, or teach them patience. BUT it would be cool to hear more people saying they wanted an internship because it was a smart steppingstone to their dream job AND that the manager was someone they admired because they exuded character traits that they hoped to learn about or gain for themselves.

After reading and discussing Brooks' book, I was not ultimately convinced that resume virtues are bad and that those growing their resumes were somehow amoral.

I believe you can pursue both, and in pursuit of both one of the great challenges people may find is how to achieve resume virtues without compromising eulogy virtues. If you look around, we need our eulogy virtue seekers to be the ones who pursue big tasks, important roles, and grow into leadership roles—the kind who tend to look good on resumes.

A scale achieves balance when parts are equal, rather than one side dominating another. If you could only have one, then it would be a shame to pick resume over eulogy virtues. But an either/or solution is an unsatisfying one to me.

So, in pursuing resume or eulogy virtues, I choose to see it not as an either/or proposition; instead, I declare it to be a both/and imperative. Perhaps the balanced approach on our road to personal development is to live in the pursuit of outstanding character and an equally outstanding resume.

Learning happens everywhere

Because of this, I often urge my students to get purposefully involved on campus and in their communities. Making the dean's list is great. Equally important to learning everything possible in the textbooks and the classroom is to learn all you can from the residence hall about dignifying all persons and being neighborly, as well as on the intramural field about being the consummate teammate and competing with both vigor and class.

I have taught in the classroom for over a decade. During that time, and even before, I have worn many hats on a college campus—advising fraternities, leading orientations, welcome-weeks, and even living-in and managing residence halls (yes, living in "the dorms" with my family and college students!).

The sheer volume of opportunities for learning *outside* of class far surpasses the opportunity for learning inside a classroom. There is no debate about it. A full-time student is in the classroom roughly 12-18 hours a week. The rest of the week they are somewhere else, and, whether intentionally or not, they are learning something. They may be gaining exceptional tools for living, or they may be developing less-than-admirable traits.

Either way, they are getting an education on living. As adaptive mammals, how can we not be constantly learning? Even the lazy, couch-potato is *learning*, even if only bad habits for living. So, the question for each day is not "are you learning and gaining," BUT "are you maximizing your learning and becoming the best version of you that you can be?" And toward that end, it's more than just reading the right books and acing courses.

CRUCIAL CONVERSATIONS

And what about you—how focused are you on resume virtues, eulogy ones, or both?

What about your lifestyle specifically demonstrates that you are maximizing your learning and becoming the best person you can be?

How can you be even more intentional about your daily living, to ensure that you cultivate lifestyle habits that will make your future-self proud?

......

Want to share this conversation with Trey, or perhaps even see your thoughts in a future version of this book?

Go to treyguinn.com/adulting and share!

Is the exchange rate for the world your soul?

The ideas brought forward in the *Road to Character* about resume versus eulogy virtues add some color to a question posed in the Christian Gospels that has always stuck with me. What good is it to gain the world if you lose your soul in the process? I wrestled with this passage as a kid because I could not fully understand it.

I think some people might hear the question as if there is a grandiose deal to be made with the devil – you can be crazy rich and world famous in exchange for your invisible soul. In which case, I believe there'd be a good number of takers who would shake hands and sign on the dotted line. After all, having never seen their soul, they may decide it might as well not exist, much less be theirs.

As I consider the passage, I can't help but search for the meaningful takeaway for me today. This is my natural inclination when receiving a message. From a daily scripture to every email in my inbox, I am always inquiring, "why does this matter?" and "what do I do with this?"

So, when I hear that phrase about gaining the world in exchange for my soul, I've got to break it down to something practical and relevant for me today. For starters, what is a soul? Google results reference the soul to be the essence of a person, the moral nature, character, etc.

So, the question becomes something like: what would I exchange for my character? Would I exchange my morals, character, beliefs and values for all the riches this world offers? Again, not super-helpful. I can hardly fathom a day when a pitchfork-holding devil would stand before me like a genie granting all my wishes in exchange for an immaterial me – *Ok Trey, last chance. Hand me your character and then you can live like a king.*

It is an odd proposition to process. Instead, there must be something about this passage that can inform my daily living. So, I start thinking about my day. Rather than a big decision like all the world for my soul, what about little decisions. In middle school, is swiping a pack of gum from the convenience store worth knowing that you are a thief? As a high schooler, is copying your friend's homework worth knowing you are a cheat?

By comparison to the whole world for your immaterial soul dilemma, these micro-decisions seem miniscule. But what if they aren't? What if it's all the same?

A soul for some shower-gel?

The door to our dorm room opens and my best friend is standing right before me.

(BEN) "Hey, got out of class early. Want to grab lunch?"

I stood still, frozen, like I had just seen a ghost.
How do I play it off? Oh, shoot. I can't. I could faint. Say something. I can't.

(ME) "Dude, I am so sorry. I don't know what to say... This is embarrassing. I'm so sorry."

Here is what happened. It was the middle of our first semester in college. We both lived three hours from home. Ben had a sizeable budget. Me, not so much. I was running out of shower-gel, and my nearly depleted supply needed to last me until winter break. In a snap judgment, I made the poor decision that my roommate—the one with the sizeable budget and habit of refurnishing his toiletries and food supply regularly—could spare the occasional squeeze of shower-gel from his shower tote.

No harm, no foul. We are the best of friends; so why would it even matter, right? And he would not have cared, especially if I had just *asked* to borrow. But I did not ask. And I kept "borrowing" for a couple weeks until that one fateful Tuesday morning.

Wrapped in a towel and with my shower tote on my arm, I am standing at the sink and just moments from leaving our room for the community showers. As one last order of business, I perform a quick and greedy squeeze of Ben's shower-gel onto my green shower scrubber.

As I kneel to put the shower-gel back into the shower tote of its lawful guardian, my best friend has opened the door and is standing inches from me. Unaware in that moment of the crime just committed against him, he proceeded to invite a dummy to lunch.

He didn't know that his best friend just made the world's worst deal.

I had exchanged a piece of my soul for a squeeze of shower-gel.

Always fail forward

Ben never cared that I used his shower-gel. Once he sized up the scene, he laughed and even felt bad for me. Even during my profuse apology, he just kept laughing and said something like, "Seriously, Guinn? It's no big deal. Why don't I just buy you one next time I'm at the store?" Then he said to stop apologizing and shower fast so that we could beat the cafeteria crowd.

It ate at me for weeks. If ever I brought it up, he laughed, and then looked at me shocked that I was still apologizing. With enough time to forgive myself, I learned to laugh about it with him. Ben and I have retold that story to ourselves and countless others over meals, on vacations, and even during weddings toasts.

It's a crowd favorite that would make for must-see tv. But privately, it has always been fuel for me. Like an athlete who watches footage from a game-missed shot or a fumbled ball, I view it as a failure that I never want to relive.

Twenty years later, and I have never laughed about that story the way he does, or the way others do. To him, and everyone else, it is just another silly college story. To me, it became a critical learning moment.

It was a moment for me when the message about *gaining the world in exchange for my soul* really sunk in. You see, I had compromised my character – and was stealing from a friend – to save less than a buck on shower gel.

I learned an enormous lesson in life. Thankfully, my friend loved me enough to forgive and laugh about it. I prayed hard about that silly situation and decided that I wanted to come out of it a better person. I wanted this embarrassing compromise of character to be a refining moment, not a defining one.

Choose to let your lapses in judgment refine you, not define you.

When new opportunities to compromise my character present themselves, I remember my failure moments like that greedy squeeze of shower-gel onto my shower scrubber and the feeling of that door opening. For those moments when we fumble the ball or make choices that call to question our character, what's done is done.

Following a moment of failure, don't curse it; learn from it. Learn so that you don't make the same mistake twice. And don't just learn from *that* mistake, learn how to rise up after *any* mistake.

You will fumble the ball again, and the stakes might be higher. Train yourself to be the person who owns it and gets back on your feet, no matter the circumstances.

My greedy squeeze of Ben's shower gel was but one failure of many for me in this lifetime. And I needed that humbling moment to learn and grow, realize the cost of my character, and discover for myself how to be refined by mistakes, and not defined by them. These can be some of the hard moments in life.

It's kind of like bombing an exam even if you studied. But just like you don't quit college or consider yourself a moron over one bad exam, never throw in the towel on your character or allow yourself to be labeled a bad person because of a poor choice or shameful situation.

On the road to character, all of us will fail a few quizzes along the way. The point is to learn as we go. I am striving to grow my eulogy virtues, not just my resume. To treat all of life as opportunity for learning, not just a classroom. To forgive myself when I fail….and to never-ever swap a piece of my soul for anything, much less a squeeze of shower gel.

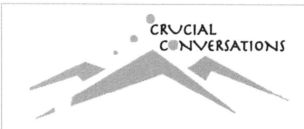

CRUCIAL
CONVERSATIONS

What about you—have you had an embarrassing failure moment? Ever been caught with your hand in the proverbial cookie jar (or shower tote as in my case)?

What have you learned and how have you grown from the times you missed the mark or fumbled the ball?

Why do you think we tend to let failures be defining?

And how can we make our failures more refining, rather than allowing them to be defining?

What critical moments in your life do you believe have been most important for your character development?

What is a character trait you hope to strengthen in the days to come?

......

Want to share this conversation with Trey, or perhaps even see your thoughts in a future version of this book?

Go to treyguinn.com/adulting and share!

Trey Guinn

PART 2

HOW YOU RELATE

Adventures in Adulting

CHAPTER 5

YOU ARE THE COMPANY YOU KEEP

"Turns out not where but who you are with that really matters."

- *David J. Matthews*

From the hallway I hear her say,

> "Do I have to?
> ...because I really don't want to
> ...how about just one page?"

That was my daughter working the angles to avoid sitting down and reading.

It had become a semi-regular conversation in our house, and I would usually try a variety of angles myself, such as: "Honey, how about you grab a book and come sit with Daddy for some family reading time?" And even the occasional bribery, "What if we all read for thirty minutes and then we can go get some ice cream?"

My tactics were normally met with a not-so-subtle rolling of the eyes, momentary compliance, light huffing, and eventually, "I don't want to do this. It's so boring… Are we done yet?"

Let the record show that I do not believe that forcing a kid to read is good for much of anything. Same goes for forcing a child to clean their room, brush their teeth, read a particular book, and all those other things parents want kids to do. So, in parenting, I try to check myself and see that first I am actively modeling the very thing I am hoping they do. Do they actually see me reading? Making my bed? Brushing my teeth? And am I taking the time to not just tell them what we should do, but also why we should do it?

Side note: parenting really is hard work. If you have not done so recently, I implore you to contact a parent or caregiver who has loved you well and tell them thank you!

As a parent, I can tell you that one of the hardest things for me is coming to grips with the reality that there are limits to my actual influence. You love 'em hard and teach 'em all you can, but ultimately everyone chooses their own adventure. I have been warned repeatedly that this happens, usually by phrases like, "When your kid leaves the nest, you just gotta let go and trust they are ready to fly."

There are at least two things that I have learned in this regard. First, as an adult-child, I have returned to the nest multiple times for love, support, and a word of wisdom from parents and those who have played a parent-like role in my life. So, one might fly the nest, but in most cases, you can return regularly for a meal, hug, and word of advice.

Second, as a parent, I have learned that leaving the nest happens regularly, and way before a kid graduates high school or some other traditional indicator that a kid is about to take flight from the nest. Actually, the moment my daughter came home from kindergarten using words I did not teach her, singing songs I had never played for her, and asking questions about things I had never brought up in her presence, I knew that in some way or another she was venturing from the nest.

Now, in the throes of elementary school, my daughters still "live" at home, but it is clear to me that much of their lives are already being lived outside of home. Much of their attitudes, beliefs, and behaviors are being informed by their peers at school, on sports teams and other extra-curricular activities, during church retreats and summer camps, and beyond.

Both of my daughters are under the age of ten, yet so much of who they are—their attitudes, beliefs, and behaviors—is forming outside the nest. And this can be totally scary to highly invested parents. At minimum, it is an exercise in faith.

The Potter and the clay

If you don't know this about me, I have an odd affinity for my neighborhood pool. It's on my running route, and during the off-season months, I smile each day when I pass by it. With impatience for pool season to begin, I occasionally see the owner around town, and remind him that I am just a short jog away if ever he needs me to hop the fence, take a dip and check the temp. You know, just help keep an eye on the place.

On opening day, I walk around like a kid in a candy store. The snack shack workers once named a drink after me. Order a "big papa" and tell them Trey sent you. Not even kidding.

Well, on a recent trip to my beloved neighborhood pool, the lifeguard blew the whistle for adult swim, sending all the kids out of the pool. My oldest daughter and her friend made a beeline for the snack shack to get ice cream bars. When they made it back to the cabana to eat them, my daughter's friend leaned down to reach into her pool bag. She gleefully pulled out her well-loved copy of *Harry Potter,* and began reading.

I acted as if I hadn't noticed but looked to the sky and silently thanked God. Why? Because right there in that very moment, I knew it would be a matter of days before my daughter was asking me for her own copy of *Harry Potter*. And, just before bed that night, she did.

One day, reading was something boring that Daddy wanted her to do. The next day, she's asking to stay up a little longer on a school night so she can finish the next chapter.

"Daddy, please, just like five more minutes 'til the end of this chapter…"

Oh, how sweet the sound.

Something had happened. My daughter did not have a mental growth spurt that caused a hunger for reading. Nor did I master the art of parenting overnight. Only one thing happened. A critical influencer in her life was reading. Now, she was too.

My daughter is not special in this regard. Neither is her friend. The story of the book at the pool is nearly one small example of what humans everywhere do regularly. Each of us, at times, are like potters—who we are shapes the world around us and consequently influences the company we keep. At other times, we are like clay—the company we keep influences us and shapes the world as we know it.

This is not just kid stuff. It's throughout life. Eventually, my daughter will be in junior high, where I can only pray the influence of her friends is positive like her friend at the pool who inspired her to read.

Speaking of middle school, I inconveniently recall that amongst other things, there was the era of the braided belt. Oh ya, you read that right: braided belts. Until middle school, they were a nonissue in my life. And if you care to know how I really feel about them, then they should have stayed that way.

But one day, walking through the cafeteria, I spotted a couple of braided belts being worn by two guys in the grade above me. We had strict dress codes, but accessories like belts were apparently a free-for-all, and these guys were flaunting their new belts with peculiar tie-and-hang style.

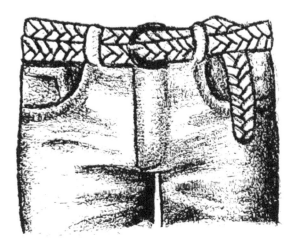

They walked around like they had just invented the moonwalk.

To me, the whole thing looked ridiculous. But by the end of the week, my friend was wearing one. And, even worse, my crush got one too, and decided to rock her tie-and-hang braided belt over a denim skirt.

Well, that was enough. That weekend, I was at the mall picking out a braided belt that was two sizes too long. After all, this is what the people in my social circle did now.

While it may illustrate the point well, to say *you are the company you keep* means a lot more than a child's reading habits and a teenager's poor fashion choices.

In fact, I have come to realize that who you surround yourself with and choose to do life with is massively important for the duration of your time on this earth.

The good of community

Community can be good and have a positive effect on individuals. This seems like an easy argument to make. But just how good and positive may surprise you. An ongoing study of more than 80 years shows that embracing community helps us live longer and happier lives.

The original Harvard Study of Adult Development began in 1938 during the Great Depression. Part of the original recruits even included President John F. Kennedy. The study has expanded to include offspring and their spouses. These researchers have discovered some rich findings that all of us can learn from, and the key takeaways can be seen in a TED talk, *What Makes a Good Life*. Some key findings reported by Professor Robert Waldinger are that "Loneliness kills. It's as powerful as smoking or alcoholism," and that "The key to healthy aging is relationships, relationships, relationships."

I agree wholeheartedly. More than money or fame, it is the quality and closeness of our relationships that keep us happy throughout our lives. Our social ties—the company we keep—protect us from life's hardships and discontents, help us delay mental and physical decline, and are better predictors of long and happy lives than social class, IQ, or genetics.

The data does not lie, and my own lived experiences confirm that we are wired to be in relationship with others, and the closer and more satisfying all the better. Yet my own research suggests that some of us are more equipped than others for making and maintaining social relationships.

The importance of doing your friendship work

Shortly after completing my Ph.D., I was offered a professorship in my hometown of San Antonio, Texas. My family and I bought a house near campus, and we made the move home. In my first week on the new job, I was setting up my office and figuring out the important stuff like where to get coffee and how to check my mail.

Low and behold, I had my first visitor. Lauren stopped by my office to introduce herself and announce that she was my newest advisee. I knew how to advise students, but didn't know what the advising protocol was at my new institution. So, I just focused on a few standard, get-to-know-you questions with the idea that I would learn her story, and then figure out the technical advising stuff after she left.

Lauren shared that she recently transferred to our university from another university that was about a three-hour drive away. Without a moment delay, I reassured her, "I am sure that your professors and friends from your former college miss you greatly, but I am glad you are here, and I look forward to knowing you."

Note: Portions of this section about doing friendship work have appeared in articles for *The Logos*, a university newspaper, and *About Campus*, which was published in partnership with ACPA and by Wiley.

Lauren paused a second, laughed slightly, and replied, "I hardly think anyone back there knows or will figure out that I left." And there was an awkward pause followed by a warm smile. I understood her quite clearly. She said it with a laugh. However, I knew with certainty that this situation was painful, not funny. Two years of her life had been lived on a campus where she felt no sense of community.

She packed her bags, loaded her car, and drove to a new college, convinced that no one had noticed her leaving. She transferred from her former institution without a single friend but with enough credits to classify as a junior.

Lauren's story is sad but not shocking. There are many people who enroll in college and miss out on making friends. I am thinking about a sophomore I met last year. He has transferred colleges twice already, is unsettled on his major, and seems to pick his course schedule with the sole purpose of minimizing his time on campus and maximizing his time at home holding a video game console.

I am also reminded of a very intelligent student I met last spring just before her graduation. She lived on campus all four years, but could not recall the name of her resident assistant or one friend she made down the hall.

Some of these students carry on fine and graduate after a few years. But the findings from my own research, and that of others, leads me to believe that making friends is one of the single best predictors of a joyful and successful college experience. Put another way, not making friends is one of the most critical predictors for why students do poorly in college and, in some cases, drop out altogether.

So, while most people will stress that in order to graduate you must hit the books and do all your schoolwork, I am here to remind that in college and beyond we must do our "friendship work" too. The good news is that friendship work is fun. And for those who want to make it rain friendship, I prescribe the following: get involved with a group and invite people to hang out. Let me explain.

The easiest way to make friends is to seek and select purposeful group involvement, such as joining a social club or becoming involved with a service group. Doing this increases your likelihood for interactions that may result in new friendships. A bonus is that the people in your newfound group will share at least one common interest with you, and that will make starting a conversation that much easier. If you both joined the local chess club, then chances are you both like chess. And that's check, mate.

For those who need to do some critical friendship work, at the top of the to-do list is to get involved with a group of people who align with your values and interests.

Additionally, inviting people to hang out, such as asking a neighbor or person who sits next to you to grab lunch or play a game of pick-up basketball, is critically important for developing friendship, sharing activities, and spending time together. Some people are scared to issue invitations. I had a former advisee who wanted friends so badly, but he had a major fear of putting himself out there and potentially being rejected.

I shared a couple of thoughts with him. First, I reminded him of a simple fact that all of us want the same thing — to have friends and feel a sense of belonging and connectedness.

Second, I pointed him to piles of research showing people are socially attracted to those who demonstrate confidence and a willingness to initiate communication. This means whether you are new to a community or facing a new year with fresh faces all around, it is to your advantage to be the one who breaks the ice and invites others to hang out.

While rejection is possible, odds are that harnessing some confidence and issuing an invitation will only enhance your social status, thus increasing the likelihood someone would want to spend time with you.

Now, some may think that doing friendship work is not for them. They might say, "Yeah, but I don't have time because I work." Or, they might think they don't need to worry about making friends in a new environment because they already have a ton of old friends or keep up with a lot of people from back home. This is faulty reasoning, especially for a college student or someone new to a community, because a joyful and successful experience within it is not realized until you become part of that community. And you are not really part of a community until you begin establishing new friendships and a social life in it. Doing so makes us happier and feel more connected. For college students, it increases the likelihood they will stay in school and helps prepare them for life after school.

So, remind people you know facing a change that from time to time they should set aside the books and "real work" in order to do their friendship work. After all, if we are the company that we keep, who are we if we keep no company?

In ancient days, long before social media and smart phones, I was a young person who went off to college. And I had my own issues to wrestle with, like who am I really and whose company ought I keep?

A life of my own

My high school graduating class was about 75 people— many of them I had known since kindergarten or early elementary. Our teachers knew us well. Sure, some kids may have been getting into some trouble. Most of us, however, were well-mannered and avoided music with cursing.

I left town and headed for college with a sense of limitlessness, no fear, and feeling ever-ready to cannonball into my new life. A life of my own. This was new for me. Growing up, I never moved cities or started a new school. I had no clue what might happen along this journey into adulting. As best I could tell, I could do anything I wanted to do, and be anyone I wanted to be. And so, within reason, I did everything and met everyone. In a new place with new people, without any reputation preceding me, what would I do, who would I be, and how would others perceive and receive me? The fact that I did not have answers to these questions was not haunting or scary. It was incredibly freeing and exciting.

I hit a dilemma, however. It was the season of fraternity rush—a time where fraternity members start hanging out with freshman and other new college guys to see if they ultimately are a good fit for their particular fraternity. I can skip explaining any further, as the Hollywood version of fraternity life is far more entertaining than mine would be. Suffice it to say, it was nearing the end of my first semester in college, and I had a tough decision to make about which fraternity to rush and pledge. In that season, this seemed like a huge dilemma. I narrowed it down to two groups, but needed help. So, I called my best friend who attended the university about 90 minutes away. I explained my dilemma and the two groups as best I knew how.

She listened patiently and supportively. Then, she offered something like the following: "I see the dilemma. Both are cool groups, and both seem to fit your personality. But one of them fits your heart and the core of who you are. And knowing you, that is the group that you will be proud to have been a part of not, just during college, but well after college. When I hear you talking about them, it's the same way I talk about you." My dilemma was over. I did not need to see or hear anything else. My best friend had just taken my hand and guided me through a slight fog.

CRUCIAL CONVERSATIONS

And what about you— have you ever been in a season when you needed to do some extra friendship work?

What methods do you believe to be the best for making quality friendships?

What are some ways this week and month that you can do meaningful friendship work? How might this impact your life positively?

I needed help making a tough decision about which group to join in college, and had a friend guide me through that decision. When have you needed some friendly guiding through a fog? Who did you turn to? What was that experience like?

If facing a fog tomorrow, who would you let take you by the hand and guide your way?

......
Want to share this conversation with Trey, or perhaps even see your thoughts in a future version of this book?

Go to treyguinn.com/adulting and share!

The company you keep is mission critical to your life, because they become who you turn to in those moments of confusion or fog, when you lose your way, or perhaps lose someone or something you love.

When I faced my mini-dilemma freshman year in college, I didn't turn to the cutest gal in my class or the most popular guy on my hall. Rather, I turned to my most trusted friend—the person I did life with. And, ironically, I was seeking help about what group of people I should be doing life with.

Ripple effects of community

The power of the company you keep really does multiply itself. The attitudes, beliefs, and behaviors you incorporate as your own come from the company you keep, and then also from the company they keep.

Case in point. Consider that Greg and Ben are best friends who happen to not drink booze, and they have plenty of fun without drinking. But then Ben starts a job where his colleagues all go for a few drinks after work. Before long, Ben is a regular drinker. And now, when Ben hangs out with Greg, he is always pouring him a drink and insisting that Greg give booze a shot. No pun intended. It's awkward because Greg loves Ben, but isn't a fan of drinking, which has clearly become a part of Ben's lifestyle. How might this influence Greg and Ben's friendship?

Or this one: Pete and Alfredo weren't runners. Alfredo's girlfriend got him hooked on jogging with her after work. Before long, Alfredo convinced Pete to join them after work for jogs in the park. Pete hated it at first but tried a few more times. Now, months later, it is Pete who constantly invites Alfredo to go running. He even signed up for a marathon.

And, for dramatic effect, I repeat: the power of the company you keep multiplies. The attitudes, beliefs, and behaviors you incorporate as your own come from the company you keep, and then also from the company they keep.

Like hikers on the mountain of life

Indeed, we are the company we keep, and at times, our lives resemble the company our company keeps. At times, this is great. At times, not so much. I faced a situation in school that was a little sad and difficult.

I made a friend at a holiday party some years ago, and we became immediate best buddies. Within a week, we were running and working out together daily. We did church together. We laughed about little things. We talked about heavy stuff. We were as close as friends can be, and it stayed this way for a couple years. At one point he moved houses, and I would go over and help him fix the place up. We always found a fun project, something that needed fixing, and it was a great excuse to get together.

Before long, he made friends with his neighbor. Turns out that guy was really into smoking pot and introduced it to my best buddy. Before long, they were smoking together daily. My friend went from non-smoker to daily smoker fast. And he was convinced that if I just gave it a try that I would like it too. And perhaps I would have, but I was not interested in smoking, and did not want to find out whether or not I'd like it.

I love him and do not judge that he smokes. The problem is that this forced a fork in the road, because truth be told, there were some real changes in the guy after just a few months. His lifestyle, daily habits, and outlook on life looked and felt noticeably different.

Our once shared activities and routines slowly fell off his schedule. Smoking his neighbor's dope and working on the house became his perfect day. But it wasn't mine. He really liked who he was becoming, and I was happy for him, but his new path was no longer aligned with mine. Like hikers on a trail, we hit a point where our paths diverged.

On the mountain of life, we come across people who we choose to hike with for one reason or another. And for a time, his was the company that I chose to keep, but our lives no longer aligned. This happens, and when it does, we have to make choices about whether to continue hiking together or part ways.

Parting ways with my friend was hard. I wanted things to stay the same, just like I am sure he wanted me to be cool with shifting our routine to one of me coming over to smoke weed with him and the neighbor. It was not the first or last time I've had to part ways with a friend or fellow hiker.

My own philosophy on this is that you must be true to yourself and the core of who you are. If you must part ways with a hiking buddy, do so peacefully and with love, never judgment.

For this reason, years later, even though my friend and I no longer do life together, we can still call or text to share good news or a life update. We pick up and laugh together as though we never parted, but we know that we chose to hike different paths. And that's ok. Life goes on.

One of my earliest lessons in hiking came on that day I told you about earlier—the call with my friend who helped me to solve the dilemma of which fraternity to join. My friend spoke the truth I needed to hear. The wisdom I heeded that day, and have held onto since, is that many people will share your hobbies, and perhaps even have a similar personality as you, but fewer will share the core of who you are. Learning some new hobbies can be cool, but compromising your core is not. So, have fun with people who share your hobbies and have a similar personality as yours, and amongst those, find the individuals who share your deeply held beliefs and values. And hold on tight because those are the ones whose company to keep.

The Harvard study is right: embracing community helps us live longer, happier lives. And like studying *the right way* leads to good grades, making *the right friends* is part of winning at life.

What about you—can you recall a situation when a friend's habits rubbed off on you in a positive or negative way? And vice versa, when have you influenced others around you in a positive or less than ideal way?

In what actual and meaningful ways are the company you currently keep (and perhaps the company they keep) shaping your life right now?

If in fact "it turns out not where but <u>who you are with </u>that <u>really matters</u>," whose company should you seek to keep and why?

Have you ever had an experience where you had to part ways with a hiking buddy? Why did you part ways and what was that experience like?

......
Want to share this conversation with Trey, or perhaps even see your thoughts in a future version of this book?

Go to treyguinn.com/adulting and share!

CHAPTER 6

YOU (RE)DISCOVER
WHAT IT MEANS TO LOVE

"Love is all you need."

-     *The Beatles*

It was a dinner party at the Guinn house. Following a nice meal, eight of us gathered in the living room to enjoy cocktails, share stories, savory sweets, and lots of laughter. A Beatles playlist in the background was hardly noticed until a guest pointed to the sound system as if to suggest we all pay attention to the wisdom in the words. The Fab Four serenaded us, "All you need is love. Love is all you need."

Having observed some sentimental smiles around the room, I saw this as the perfect opportunity to raise my glass and share a few words.

Can you picture it? Like a scene from a movie, all the happy people with food and drink in hand. I stood with one hand in my blazer and another holding my drink. I locked eyes with my friends and was seconds from saying a dad-like comment about God's goodness and how grateful I am for the opportunity to share this time together. But, before I could murmur a single word, the moment was gone; all was upside-down.

"All you need is *love*. Now, that is just plain ridiculous," one of our guests said. My glass went down as quickly as I could register her words.

A moment of awkward silence was broken, but painfully so, when her husband retorted, "What is *more* important than love?" The couple went back and forth on this for a few minutes. The rest of the room was eyeing the conversation in hopes that it would turn to something funny. But nervous laughter quickly turned to phone checks and offers to pick up plates and do dishes.

Note: Parts of the story, "All you need is love," previously appeared in an article I wrote for *The Logos*, a university newspaper.

And then one guest—who shall remain nameless— humorously suggested, "Trey teaches this stuff. Maybe he should settle the debate."

An awful idea, I thought. Please, Lord, not now. Make my phone ring and let it be urgent. I dodged the lover's quarrel as best I could. But as it turned out, the one piece of common ground the couple could find was that they both wanted me to weigh in on their argument. I ultimately obliged and will share here a few of the thoughts I shared with them that night.

If people don't agree on the problem, then it will be nearly impossible for them to agree on the solution. Savvy businesspeople understand this principle. Getting people in a boardroom to agree on a solution is hard enough—much harder when they don't all agree on the actual problem they are proposing to solve. You must first agree on the problem(s) before moving forward together on a solution. Similarly, this couple was debating whether "love" is all a relationship needs. And my hunch was that the crux of their debate was in how each of them individually defined the term "love." So, I asked them, "When you hear those lyrics, what does the word 'love' mean to you?"

For the wife, it meant passion and feelings of being "in love," a definition closely aligned with the ancient Greek term, "Eros." Think cupid and all the falling-in-love stuff.

Her husband, however, described love differently. "To say I love you," he explained, "means that I am committed to you, want to spend time with you, and do nice things for you." His was very much a love of chosen commitment—I chose you then and I choose you forever, for better or worse, and until death do us part.

Once they said these things out loud, it was quite obvious this argument was merely a matter of definition. They would never have solved this quarrel about whether *love* is all you need without first coming to an agreement over the definition of the word itself.

A theory of love developed by Robert Sternberg offers that the stages and types of love that people experience in a relationship depends on three components: intimacy (e.g., feelings of closeness and connectedness), passion (e.g., feelings of adoration and attraction), and commitment (e.g., the decision to remain together for the long haul).

Whereas an ideal relationship that most couples strive toward would have a surplus of all three components (which is called consummate love), a relationship based on only one element is less likely to survive.

In the example above, the wife was defining love as passionate arousal. So, according to her definition of love, she is right. Romantic passion is not all we need. In fact, passion without intimacy and commitment leads to a type of puppy love that is likely to dissolve sooner than later.

Even healthy relationships may not experience consummate love—which consists of all three components—forever. For instance, couples can enter a period of life in which feelings of passion toward one another wane. Ever heard people talk about the seven-year itch or losing that loving feeling? Such a relationship might be identified as having dissolved into a "companionate love;" lacking passion and comprised of intimacy and commitment only.

For some couples, this is reason enough to cut ties and jump ship. They may not flirt together as they used to, and you might hear them say, "We still love each other, but we've just lost that spark."

For some, waning passion is reason to do whatever necessary to generate a love-spark through activities such as making time for a date night or taking up a special hobby together.

Others consider waning passion to be a typical evolution in a relationship, like changing seasons. We were hot and now we are cold, but maybe we'll heat up again in time.

To complicate things further, feelings of love and attraction bloom in many different ways and is not always logical. You might crush on your doctor in the examination room or your professor in the classroom, but if you randomly met that same person on the aisle of your grocery store, you might not even take a second look.

Same goes for your work crush. At work, the person seems to awaken your attraction, but under a different context—say just one more person you met at a social last weekend—would they really grab much of your attention?

Why might these scenarios be true? It may seem crazy to read at first, and perhaps you wish to dismiss altogether, but I dare you to stop and actually think about it.

Attraction is a funny thing and can be instigated by a number of variables. Your heart may race with passionate love for that really cute person you met last week. You may crave your celebrity crush when you hear their song on the radio (much like a kid craves a Happy Meal when they see golden arches). Most often, taste buds will change and crushes fade, but that is not always the case. Time with a crush can be a total disappointment, or it can be the start of something more. Time together may reveal shared interests and values that prompt genuine friendship.

Unlike relationships that start as romantic attraction, are those that grow in the garden of friendship. I am reminded of the numerous couples I have known over the years who met in class or in a student organization, started studying or volunteering together, and developed a respect for the other person that evolved into a true friendship. Before too long, or perhaps a decade later, one of them is stopping by my office and flashing an engagement ring in my face.

Romantic relationships form any number of ways. My observations and lived experiences have led me to believe that the garden of friendship is a safe place to grow sustaining love.

To say that a romantic relationship grew in the garden of friendship is not to say that two people found each other unattractive, became friends, and then said, "Well, he's cute enough." It could work that way, but I am actually referring to instances when the connection between two people was a friendship first, regardless of any physical attraction. I would not argue that it is the one and only way to enter romance, but for many people it has been a safer, smarter, and successful path toward consummate love.

About (re)discovering love

We continue to (re)discover and (re)define love throughout our lives. If unsure what I mean by that, for a moment, think about the body and all its muscles. Now, you may be like me and exercise regularly. By that, I mean I run every day about four miles or so. Nothing to scoff at, but nothing too strenuous either. It would be easy to assume that because one exercises *every* day that they know a lot about health, fitness, muscles, etc., but this is not true. Make me do your swim routine tomorrow or take me water-skiing this weekend, and the soreness in my body the day that follows will prove that there are many muscles that I have forgotten about or have not yet met before.

Similarly, I love to cook for my family. Each day, I get in the kitchen, turn on the news or a favorite playlist, and cook away. This is part of my daily routine and I make a few dishes quite well, but I am no expert on cooking. And this is because there are many countries I have never traveled, cultures I have never encountered, and cuisines I have never tasted. So, while I run and cook every day, I am far from a fitness expert or master chef.

As we discover new things, whether muscles in our body or world cuisines, we come to understand and define things differently. At minimum, we come to realize that there is much we do not know. Bono, the lead singer of U2, put it quite well in a song that goes, "The more you see the less you know. The less you find out as you go. I knew much more then than I do now."

Now, I can't argue that I know what he meant by this. But I know what it means to me when I hear him sing it. The bigger your world gets the smaller you become. The more you learn about this vast world, the more aware you become that your understanding of it is smaller than you thought. It's perfectly humbling and enriching.

Puppies in/and love

This reminds me of a time in class that was slightly painful but ultimately beautiful. It was a graduate seminar I was teaching on relationship research. One night in particular, we were discussing relational dissolution; meaning breakups, divorces, and that stuff. A few minutes into the discussion of readings, a young man in the class declared his disapproval of divorce and asked why we should even be talking about it (as if our discussion somehow gave credence to this cultural phenomenon).

A retired veteran in the class exclaimed that regardless of whether we like it or not, divorce is a part of life for many and worthy of our studying. Well said, I thought, and so I stayed quiet and let the students lead the discussion. This back and forth got a little tense, and it became even more so when, following the veteran's disclosure that she had been divorced, the young man decided to re-enter the discussion, but this time with scripture to bolster his views. At this, I was ready to declare a 10-minute break. But I didn't need to. The veteran responded with exceptional grace and shared that she knew those scriptures well. She explained that she had recited them to herself numerous times, particularly when trying to endure the alcoholism, cheating, and physical abuse of her spouse.

She politely suggested that she and the young man agreed very much in principle, but that life had presented her some new obstacles that required an evolving understanding for how to navigate her experience, as well as a new lens through which to see and understand the life experiences of others.

Her willingness to share and to do so with such grace had been a moment for all of us, and perhaps a private concert for the young man. Like Bono singing to me, he certainly heard clearly, "The more you see the less you know." Moments before, he had been so sure of his view on divorce. The more he saw it through the eyes of another, the less he knew, and the less certain he was.

I wouldn't show up to your holiday feast and ask why you didn't include the side that my family always serves. No, I want to learn from you and experience the holiday meal through your lens. Just like visiting a new culture, I would never tell people they are cooking the food wrong. I rather take time to see how they cook their dishes, spice their foods, and actually learn from them rather than just try and fit them into my limited worldview. Learning from others and seeing the world through their eyes is much better than trying to fit the world into our limited perspective.

I believe that, in a funny way, love is like this too. Through our lived experiences, we each discover and come to define love differently over time. This is a good thing. Think about those individuals who had sad or unhealthy examples of love from their own parents. Should they pay attention only to those parents and replicate those relationships for themselves? No! But, sadly, some do.

Just as some families pass down really bad eating habits, some pass down really unhealthy relationship habits. Some habits are meant to be broken. If we can teach people to eat healthier than the food they were served at home, then we can teach people to do relationships better than they saw done at home.

Like the young man in my graduate seminar who quoted scripture to impose his desire that we not discuss divorce, I appreciate hearing a teenager wail about the meaning of romantic love or a twenty-year old in my classroom make passionate claims about a particular facet of why couples should always do this or never do that.

It's like when someone giggles at teenagers holding hands and call it puppy love. Sure. It is puppy love. But puppy love *is love* to puppies.

I smile when a teenager makes passionate pleas about what is right or wrong for a relationship. I smile not in a condescending way, but because I love that they care and believe wholeheartedly that what they are saying is absolute truth. This is sweet in a way. It means they really care about the topic, which is great!

I also smile because I know that their ardent beliefs are shaped by what they know and are subject to change as they come to know more. Just like my own views have evolved and will continue to.

I don't presume a monopoly on relationship knowledge. I know only what I know now. But give me a few more years, a few more life experiences, and I'll know more. At least, I hope so!

Do not throw out love with the bath water

Sadly, I have known plenty of individuals who, upon a bad bit with romance, perhaps a bad bout of puppy love, declare to never love again. Too much spice, a burned tongue, and that is it for them. Tragic. We hardly stop eating because we got food poisoning that one time a few years ago, do we?

One can have a nut allergy or a certain intolerance that sends them to the hospital, but they don't switch to a water only diet for the rest of their life.

No, instead we accept that our life experiences sharpen us to the world around us, and henceforth we take responsibility for our diet. We avoid certain restaurants or sides of the menu, stick to only certain aisles in the grocery store, and perform whatever tests necessary for checking the heat before getting burned on the tongue again.

Each disgusting and delicious bite of food we've ever had becomes a discovery into our understanding of eating.

In many ways, love is the same.

Perhaps you have tried a dish at a potluck that you secretly spit out and thought, "That is disgusting. I would not give that to my dog." No different than a first date gone badly. And then there is that intoxicatingly rich dessert where that one bite was divine, but it is not worth having a second because it was nothing but sugar. I liken these to our cupid-crushes. Sure, a kiss would be sweet, but deep down we know that there is no potential for a substantive relationship.

I could play this analogy out all day. If you ever take a class with me, then you will discover that sometimes I do! That is not the point, however. The point, instead, is that eating is part of life. For the vast majority of us, so is romantic love. As we learn and grow, we begin to see ever more clearly the effects of our diet—how it quite literally shapes us. Similarly, the choices we make about romantic love are consequential.

But unlike eating, loving is not a one-way street

The analogous relationship of love and eating is useful but imperfect. One way it is imperfect is the presumed selfish nature of eating. We consume food for our purposes. In my humble opinion, love is not meant to be this way.

So, I encourage that we consider the analogy of food to love insomuch as it helps us think about what love can be— a shared venture rather than merely individual consumption.

What kind of love are you capable of sharing? This is a really important question to ask. I have found that love is enjoyed best when we are ripe for love. Most people don't care much for a bruised banana, much like they don't care to date a bruised romantic partner who is healing and rebounding from a hurting heart or bitter breakup.

Until you are ripe for relationship, it is best to find your companionship in trusted friends, family, and perhaps wiser others. I recall a season of my life when I had gone through a devastating breakup. I so badly wanted companionship and closeness with someone.

Romantic companionship and cuddling can feel like Aloe Vera to the sunburn of a broken heart. But there are short term gains and potentially long-term hurts that can come from seeking soothing, comforting, or affection from a romantic companion when not ripe for relationship.

Put another way, rebound relationships and hook-ups are like binge drinking but with a horrendous hangover. And for those already nursing the wounds of a break-up, it just adds insult to injury, leading people to curse relationships even more. This is fact, like saying that robbing a bank is a bad idea. No need to find out for yourself. And as the late Christopher Wallace, known professionally as The Notorious B.I.G., would say, "If you don't know, now you know."

So, is love all you need?

I believe The Beatles were on to something. I liked the song as a kid, and the older I get, the more I like the song. Now, it's more to me than fun lyrics with a catchy beat. There is wisdom in the words, and so I sing it with heart and soul. I sing it to my kids when soothing them to sleep. I sang it over my mom while holding her hand in the hospital. I smile really big and sing it loudly to my wife in the car on vacation.

For me, all good things and love originate from God. So, I thank God each day for His perfect love. I thank Him that He sent His Son to model a perfect love on this Earth for each of us, and I pray that I could learn to love as He loves.

Truly, the more I (re)discover love, the richer my understanding and definition of the word. And so yes, I believe that love is all we need.

CRUCIAL CONVERSATIONS

What about you—how do you define love? Is it all you need? Why or why not?

What do you believe constitutes a loving relationship?

How has your understanding of love been (re)defined over time?

. . . . . .

Want to share this conversation with Trey, or perhaps even see your thoughts in a future version of this book?

Go to treyguinn.com/adulting and share!

PART 3

WHAT YOU DO

CHAPTER 7

YOU LET YOUR LIFE SPEAK

"Look for truth within yourself...Let your life speak."

- *Robert Lawrence Smith,*
  A Quaker Book of Wisdom

A gem of a book, *Let Your Life Speak* by Parker Palmer, was handed to me in the early 2000's by a dear friend and mentor. For its wisdom, coupled with ease of reading, Palmer's collection of essays had been chosen as the common reading for all incoming freshmen the upcoming academic year.

And I, because of my reputation for enthusiastic embrace of new projects and over-caffeinated abilities to deliver quickly, was given the task of pre-reading the book and helping develop teaching materials and discussion questions for the freshmen who would soon inherit the book and be placed in reading groups.

Over the next few months, I had the pleasure of leading freshmen seminars on Friday mornings that centered on Palmer's book. With my arms full of donut boxes and discussion handouts, I arrived each Friday ready to pass the coffee and stir the conversation. I loved facilitating those Friday mornings. As a discussion leader, phrases like "Hmm… that's interesting" and "say more about that" flew off my tongue with ease.

What I learned during those coffee-fueled and donut-filled Friday mornings struck chords that still reverb in me today. One thing learned was that we are infinite seekers of truth; each of us longing to be surer of who we are and what we are made to do. As a matter of convenience and often a curse, we don't have to look hard to find answers — *from the outside*. Parents, teachers, coaches, peers, neighbors, social media, and virtually anyone at any time eagerly send us messages about who we are and what we should do.

The wisdom in Palmer's book helps my students and me practice the art of silencing, or at least being more judicious with, the outside noise. It helps us learn to hear our own voice and listen to the inner teachings that guide us toward a sense of meaning and purpose.

My take on Palmer's book is that you are born with certain gifts and talents — perhaps you are wired creatively, scientifically, philosophically, or in some other unique and beautiful way. Over time, some people mistakenly abandon their gifts and uniqueness as they are bombarded by the influx of spoken and unspoken expectations handed down by others.

By doing so, many individuals tragically leave or set aside a sense of true self, and mold into a version of self that seems to meet the expectations held by others—sometimes attempting to mimic or even wear the mask of another in exchange for authentic self.

If this were captured in a thought bubble, it might go something like this:

Who I am is not good enough. So, rather than living to be the world's best version of myself, I better figure out how to look and act more like her.

I imagine that most people would rather not admit such thoughts exist, much less confess that they too have had such thoughts.

I have not formally studied this, but life experiences and anecdotal evidence tells me that a good many of those that suffer from something like a mid-life crisis are people that have grown tired of living someone else's life and meeting someone else's expectations.

They have found the mask to be too heavy of a burden to wear. They are ready to rip it off and reclaim their life. So, they cut their hair the way they've always wanted to and pick up the paintbrush they put down when they were 14.

What could have been their vocation at one point in time becomes, at best, a weekend hobby that they get to as schedule allows. And they say something like, "I don't know why I ever stopped [insert activity here]. It's something that has always brought me such joy."

CRUCIAL CONVERSATIONS

What about you--can you recall a time when you felt something like the thought bubble above? What specifically triggered you to think and feel this way?

What activities and experiences in your life bring you great joy and satisfaction, perhaps even a sense of purpose? Do other people in your life support and encourage you in these things? Why or why not? How does their support (or lack of support) make you feel?

What are truths about you, your unique self and giftedness, that you should never abandon?

What are the activities and experiences in your life that you should always find time for, no matter what the expectations are around you? In other words, what is the paintbrush you should never put down?

......
Want to share this conversation with Trey, or perhaps even see your thoughts in a future version of this book?

Go to treyguinn.com/adulting and share!

I had a client-meeting just last week with a nice guy who balances living between California, New York, and Mumbai. Lining up our schedules for a call is never easy! He works for a major technology company. Chances are you have one or more of their products within reach.

On our first call some months ago, he thanked me for being willing to meet on short notice, and then launched in with his dilemma. He wanted help preparing for an internal interview, especially with negotiating certain aspects of a foreseeable promotion.

While I knew that he wanted to start our call getting down to business, my gut said to pull back and hear his life story first. I said, "I promise to work fast, but first give me ten minutes to hear the real you. Set your resume aside. Tell me who you are. What makes you smile?"

He was genuinely taken aback. He seemed shocked, if not agitated for a moment, but then he began to share his story. He kept sharing, and then shared some more.

We hit the hour mark, when the call was supposed to conclude, and *I knew him*. In an hour of time, more than just interview prep, I knew that he loves dogs, reading books, and wishes to live in the remote countryside of India where he can provide a homestead for his extended family. He dreams of establishing a place where his grandchildren can come to play with his dogs and discuss philosophy and ancient wisdom.

As I sat listening to him, my heart felt heavy for a couple reasons. First, it was obvious to me that I was the first person he had shared these things with. By the end of the call, he had confirmed as much to me. On one side, I felt sad for him—to know that the life he dreams of is held in secret and on standby indefinitely. Second, it pained me to realize that the life he spoke about sounds nothing like the life he called to get help interviewing for.

We kept working together, and fast forward to the most recent call when I finally asked, "So, are these 80-hour work weeks at a job you kind of enjoy just your way of killing time honorably before finally retiring to the life you want?" And he confirmed that I was right.

After a little shock from my question and some laughing, we processed together and concluded that his career path was, by design, successful enough to please his family, and at least more interesting for him than having to be a doctor.

There is something very admirable and responsible about his path—he wants to be successful and make his parents proud. Many well-meaning young people do the same, and often they make enormous compromises for the sake of living up to the expectations and counsel of older others.

As a young person, I loved the stage and sought every opportunity possible to act and perform. Comedy, drama, musicals, crazy outfits, pounds of makeup, falling off stage to fake-dying on stage, I was up for trying anything. And in my heart of hearts, I believe that I could have been the happiest, minimum wage earning, local actor you never met.

But I heard enough people tell me too many times that acting was a fun hobby, and it was time to get off the stage and get serious about where I wanted to go to college and what I was going to do with my life.

But didn't they know? I was the lucky one that had already found at least one thing that I wanted to do with my life. I wanted to act.

What was so wrong with that? Well, I got the message loud and clear that acting was a fun extracurricular but not a serious way to live.

Aside from acting, the only images of a future self that a younger me could clearly see was being a teacher. I had some great teachers who really cared for me. The kind that make you want to be a teacher too.

I imagined myself making a classroom come alive. I envisioned teaching like an actor on a stage. The students would become part of the performance too. Or like an orchestra conductor, I saw my students as the musicians, and together we'd play the song of learning.

And this was a major bummer too, because according to some important adults in my life, "Those that can, do; those that can't teach."

I very much dislike that quote, and I always have.

I couldn't help that these thoughts about acting and teaching swam in my head. So, by the end of high school, I did not know what I wanted to become, but I heard enough from others to "know" that acting was not a *real job* and teaching was not a *good job*.

I slowly began to laugh off and let go of those childish images of myself, hoping that new adult-like images would appear. I trusted that college would do it— that in college I would discover a more glorious career path that was deemed responsible, successful, and one that would cause all humans nearby to think highly of me.

As a bit of glorious irony, it was some years later when I first began teaching Palmer's book on Friday mornings. In the practice of letting my own life speak, I not only discerned, but also came to love and accept a very real and clear call to teach.

Hotline Bling

The truth is that the call to teach never stopped ringing. I did, however, try to silence the ringer and tell them they had the wrong number.

My freshman year of college—18-year-old me—was sitting in a large lecture hall with about 200 other freshmen. The lights were dim and professor monotone. Unable to focus on a word he said, I could think only of all the fantastic ways I would do his job if given the chance.

I would open the lecture with a fun question or quote, change the lights, infuse the room with funky sounds and cool music, walk the aisles and interact with students to keep the class awake and capture the attention of my audience.

I did this for about two weeks, and then one day during a geology lecture, I casually looked up to the ceiling and asked, "Lord, why can't I pay attention?"

And, God as my witness, like it came from the Heavens, I heard back, "You are paying attention. I'm not making you into a geologist. You are becoming a teacher." I nearly cried. And not the happy tears of joy or exultation. If this was the call to teach, then I wished it were a wrong number.

I wasn't supposed to be a teacher, was I?

Most people in my family are lawyers. A successful business owner or doctor would have been fine. The message seemed clear. Study whatever you want, become something great, and law school will be your safety net.

A teacher? Perhaps God was just building in me a sense of altruism for working with youth groups on Sunday mornings. Or maybe this was a glimpse into my retired years when a successful me gets invited to speak somewhere and sign books for those aspiring to have a fabulous career like mine.

I tried to think little of it. Don't worry about job stuff, I thought. Just soak up the awesomeness of college. Really, my years as an undergraduate were exceptional. The friendships, freedom, and fun were rivaled only by the daily discoveries of new ideas and transformative learning that set me on a path as a

...lifelong learner, and a...full-time *educator*.

It happened overtime; I gave up on trying to tell myself who to be and stopped wondering how to chase a life that might please a family member or impress this or that person.

My life began to speak.
Or, rather, I began to truly listen.

I think what allowed the time and space for me to listen is when I fought the urge to always have an answer to the perennial question, "What will you become?" and started asking myself, "Who will you become?"

And rather than force what felt unnatural or network my way into places with people who didn't actually inspire me, I made time to get to know professors and people in my community who talked about things that felt important to me. I craved being around people who cared about and interacted with others in a way that resonated with me.

I realized that I did not like kissing-up to showboats and blowhards who talked about their accolades and money. It seemed to me that if I did not enjoy networking with these people, nor want their advice and counsel when trying to get an internship or job, then I probably would not want to actually work for them some day. And why would I want to be around them if I didn't want to become more like them?

So, as a college student, I prayed hard about having a circle of mentors around me—people I could trust and turn to on my journey to self. When I found someone that I admired, then I pursued time on their calendar.

By the time I graduated from college, I had developed a web of professors, university administrators, and church leaders who inspired me, shined light on me, and coached me into a better version of me.

Nearly twenty years later, most of these people are still on my speed dial. Some I talk to annually, most of them weekly, and one of them daily. During critical seasons of my life, these individuals have helped me discover the person I am becoming.

And it turns out that a clearer sense of who I am has allowed me to more earnestly pursue activities that let my life speak.

...

Sure, I think I could have been a good lawyer. I have the work ethic and drive to have made it happen, but I don't think being a lawyer would have been good for me. I can swim against the river, too. But I'd rather get in and take the time necessary to learn the natural flow of the water.

I have learned that a critical key to success is forming and maintaining relationships with great mentors. A word of caution; a great mentor will not try to mold you into their image or set you on their path—grooming you into a mini-me. Instead, great mentors help us to become more of ourselves. A great mentor will ask great questions, offer necessary support, and appropriately challenge you as you discover and pave your path.

I've had a number of students over the years come into my office, and after a few minutes, they say phrases like, "I just want to do what you do. I mean, like, how did you get to be where you are? Did you go to school for a long time or...? I mean, like, you are such a great professor and..." This is all very flattering to hear (even if the flattery is all to try warming me up before asking me for a deadline extension). Still, it is possible that some saw a guy who had some stuff figured out and seemed happy, so they wanted to know the secret. And I imagine—eh, actually know for certain—that some dear colleagues of mine are tempted to feel special when hearing stuff like this.

Let me be clear, I don't let words like this make me feel special. I feel humbled, incredibly fortunate, and immensely grateful for the life I live. At this very moment, I am sitting on my front porch with breakfast and writing a book while my kids pedal their bikes before me. This is work? Really? Yes, please! But just because my path is wonderful for me does not make it wonderful for anyone else. So, when a person asks about my path, I don't speak my life over them or hand them the roadmap to become more like me; I ask about them, and as necessary, share *how* I discovered my path and continually work to discover more of who I am becoming.

The person wrestling earnestly with the hard questions of life about who and what they will become is usually in a vulnerable spot. Giving easy answers and quick fixes may be tempting, and a flattered soul may be quick to see the destressed path-seeker and groom them into protégés, which on its face seems like a nice thing.

My best advisors and mentors, though, have never tried to form me into their image. In fact, they've urged me to discover my own path by learning all I can from theirs, but not replicating it. For this reason, I get a tad bit leery when I visit with someone who tells me how they want to be just like some particular high school coach they had or so-and-so youth minister from home.

It's great to have a referent point—a person to admire—but letting your life speak is an individual's process of self-discovery toward illuminating a pathway toward vocation and life-calling. In that process of self-discovery and illuminating the pathway, it's a true gift to have mentors and admirable others helping us onward. But the path forward must be our own.

CRUCIAL CONVERSATIONS

What about you—when have you most recently tuned out the noise around and just listened to your life?

What are some things that you have learned to be true about who you are, your inner-self, and what you were made to do with your life?

Who are the people in your life that you admire most, look to for wisdom and insight, and why?

Who are the people that you seek for mentorship? What kinds of questions are they asking you to help you discover more of yourself? And what things are they speaking into your life?

Or, what steps can you and should you be taking to find wise mentors? And why is it important that they help you discover more of yourself, rather than merely mold you into their own image?

......

Want to share this conversation with Trey, or perhaps even see your thoughts in a future version of this book?

Go to treyguinn.com/adulting and share!

CHAPTER 8

YOU WORK HARD
AT WORK WORTH DOING

*"Far and away the best prize that life has to offer is
the chance to work hard at work worth doing."*

- *Theodore Roosevelt Jr.,
  26th President of the
  United States*

I love the quote above by our former president, Teddy
Roosevelt. For starters, Roosevelt implies that to work is a
prize, which unto itself sounds counter-cultural. Many I
know are aiming for maximum days off and early retirement
from their job, if not a means to escape working altogether.

I understand where this mindset comes from. I can also enjoy some well-deserved time off, but a life of seeing work as a chore and living-for-the-weekend is hardly aspirational. Better to be someone who is both inspired by their work and equally excited for an upcoming family getaway.

Work itself can be great, but it gets a pretty bad rap, and its value is easily lost on many. We live in an increasingly attention-starved society wherein people dream of fame, long for luxuries, and (perhaps unwittingly) hand over precious hours in the day to myriad social media addictions. Under such conditions, perhaps the idea that work is a prize is a hard sell.

If we take a closer look at the quote, it seems that Roosevelt doubles down on his affinity for work. He suggests that it is not just work but the chance to work *hard* that is the real prize. I hear this being said with a pause and then emphatic ending, "… the best prize that life has to offer is the chance to work… hard!"

This implies that easy work is less of a prize than hard work. Might this be an even harder sell?

Again, that is not where this quote by President Roosevelt ends. So, let's read it again and this time imagine that the ending comes with pauses, "… the best prize that life has to offer is the chance to work… hard… at work… worth doing."

This is my favorite way to read the quote because it reflects something that I know to be true about the people I most admire. It also projects something I hope to be true about the life I am trying to live.

What is your why

I stand in agreement with President Roosevelt. And, yes, I believe that working (e.g., mowing the yard, washing the dishes) is better than a lazier alternative (e.g., eating chips and watching Netflix on the couch). Perhaps this is a bias of mine.

And I also believe that working hard, pushing yourself, and breaking a sweat when able is better than dragging your feet and slugging along. Again, perhaps a bias of mine, but I agree with the quote most when read in its entirety, because I have found that committing to the work deemed worth doing is an incredible thing.

Sometimes though, it is on us to choose a certain perspective. For example, anyone can clean house, less enjoy it, and some even choose to pay others to. I have always opted to clean my own house and do my own yard work. With a family of five, there is always cleaning to do.

At any given time, I can tell you a list of numerous chores that need completing. But before reciting *what* needs to be done, I often tell myself *why* I will do it. My wife's family is coming to town this weekend—and I want to honor them with a clean, inviting home. That's my why. So, to better love my wife and her parents (my why), today I am cleaning the house and doing yard work (my what).

This focus beyond *what* I am doing to *why* I am doing it, allows me to care for what I am doing and see the value in my work. It invites an attitudinal shift that echoes our very own President Roosevelt.

A clear and focused *why* statement makes the difference between working hard for the sheer goodness of character-building (albeit good unto itself, can also make many an eye-roll) versus working hard because the outcome has value and meaning. I love a clean home and don't mind doing the work to have one.

Plenty of times I do housework just because it needs to get done. But I frequently choose to find the why; not just the what. It makes the difference. Working hard is character-building. Working hard at worth work doing is living on purpose. Put together, this is a winning combination.

What about you—what do you think about the idea that working hard at work worth doing is a prize?

What is some *work* in your life that is prone to making your eyes roll?

How might a clear and focused why statement help you find the prize in working hard at even this work? I dare you to create a legitimate why statement, for even your most irritating example of mundane work.

· ···

Want to share this conversation with Trey, or perhaps even see your thoughts in a future version of this book?

Go to treyguinn.com/adulting and share!

Work worth doing

Last summer, my wife Shannon and I spotted a weekend in our schedule that we could pack our bags and getaway. We caught flights to her hometown of Lake Tahoe. I am under the impression that Lake Tahoe is a glimpse of Heaven, a wink from God to remind us of His majesty.

We got to town and spent our days hiking, kayaking, and running. Oh, and lots of sunrise breakfasts and sunset dinners. Throughout the trip we talked about our hopes and dreams, possible ideas of what the future might hold, and some inclinations of what we believe God is doing in our family and all around us.

Shannon has an incredible knack for listening closely. She is one of the good people, the kind who don't judge others. She just listens supportively and then occasionally asks a piercing question like, "Well, that sounds awesome. How will you get started?" This is perhaps her way of saying, "Just do it!"

On our trip last summer, she said it a lot. I shared with Shannon about an idea I had for a children's book to help teach our kids and other kids about gratitude. I shared with her about a research project that I had been dreaming of launching for years but not had the time to start or finish. I shared about how I missed acting—something really fun that I had just sort of stopped doing. And I shared about this nudging I felt that we needed to volunteer with the student ministry at church.

I went on and on. Poor thing, she must have been sick of my voice by the end of our trip! Even still, she listened patiently and lovingly throughout the weekend as we hiked, ran, and kayaked our way through her childhood stomping grounds.

And each night as we cooked dinner and ate on the beach, she would smile and convince me that all these ideas could and would come to be.

She was right. In less than a year I can take a pen and check off the things listed above and a number of others. It has required many steps to get there, but oh how fun it has been!

The first step for us was recognizing and prayerfully considering the bubbling of thoughts and ideas that wanted out. Rather than numb our inner wisdom with distractions and entertainment, sometimes we need to be diligent about creating time and space for silence, thinking, praying, and listening for inner wisdom.

It also helps to have someone in your life like Shannon, a friend and cheerleader, who loves you, listens well, and asks smart questions.

Then, you must do something with that inner wisdom. You must honor it. You must write it down and have the courage to do it!

I've always thought about a verse in the Bible that references a person who, after looking in the mirror, walks away doing nothing. I am not a theologian, and there may be infinite wisdom to the verse that I do not understand, but here is how I always took it to mean. I picture a guy with the sense and ability to get up and check himself in the mirror. He sees something that needs his attention, but he lacks the care, courage, or commitment necessary to fix what needs fixing. So, he is damned to know there is an issue he is choosing to ignore, a problem he is unwilling to fix, or an opportunity he knows about but is not seizing.

Imagine that you were on a job interview for a gig you really wanted. You are having lunch with your potential boss, and halfway through the lunch you feel something stuck between your two front teeth. You manage to get up and check yourself in the bathroom, see the piece of food lodged between your teeth, and then just walk off and do nothing about the food in your teeth.

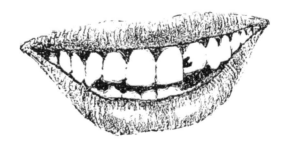

You just leave it there, stroll back to your interview, and carry on! You would never do that, right? In that case, what was the good of that inner feeling that something was between your teeth? Why did you take the time to get up and check your teeth, if you weren't going to actually do anything about it? It seems ludicrous right?

Actually, it reminds me of when I talk to someone who feels a conviction about their life – a job they need to quit, a relationship they need to end, a wellness plan they want to start, a town they are longing to move to, a college they wish to apply to, and so on. They feel it in their gut that it is what they should do. They tell you about it repeatedly. They are always serious about it this time. They sense a certain burden or consequence if they don't just do it, yet they don't do it! Like the guy that looked in the mirror and knew what to do but walked away.

Similarly, I think about all my hiking and talking with Shannon in Tahoe. All the digging into my soul, listening for inner-wisdom, and sharing for days about what I believed to be the important work worth doing.

Why would I do all that if in the end I lacked the care, courage or commitment to... *just do it?*

The courage to say yes

I've shared already that I love acting but had kissed it goodbye when I was a teenager. Well, following the hikes in Tahoe, I decided to say "yes" and put myself out there. This past year, I ended up doing a few commercials, a short film, and a few student-run productions. Also, this last week, and for the next few weeks to come, I am acting in a feature film that is being produced in Texas.

I am having a blast re-exploring acting. But that doesn't mean it isn't hard work. I mess up my lines sometimes, it demands time from my schedule, and might end up taking a toll on my body—I've got a couple fighting scenes coming up, where I will likely get roughed up a bit!

Some might wonder why I would get involved in all this anyway. Well, for starters, I want to practice what I preach. Last summer I listened to myself and heard that acting was on my mind and heart.

What remained unseen was whether I would have the courage to say yes, take first steps, and open the door to what may come. And with the encouragement of a loving wife, I chose to say yes.

I said yes to other projects too. The children's book, *Doggy Discovers Gratitude,* has been written, illustrated, and published (all credit goes to Shannon!). Find it on Amazon!

We've gone all-in with the student ministry at our church, chaperoned retreats, and I've done a little preaching too. The research project has been developed, approved, launched, and I have been collecting data for a few months now.

I could go on about various projects and opportunities that we are saying yes to. They excite us a great deal because we define it as the work worth doing. We started by taking a long look in the mirror. And we got honest about what we saw. Then, rather than walk away feeling accomplished for merely checking ourselves in the mirror, we cheered one another into the courage required to do something about what we saw.

Each of us has an inner wisdom that is ready to be heard and honored. The questions then are: Will you make the time to listen? Will you have the courage to say yes to work worth doing?

I wish that were all there is to say about work worth doing but there is much more. The courage to say yes is only one side of the coin. Harder for me, at times, is the other side of that coin.

The courage to say no

Some would say that I am the last person who should offer advice on the art of saying no. For decades I have been lovingly scolded by family, friends, and colleagues telling me that it is the one word I ought to learn. So, I share here aware that my learnings of saying no come mostly by way of failure to do so, and that I stand to learn much more.

I don't exactly know why some of us struggle with saying no, yet others express it with ease and perhaps elation. Is it a fear of missing out? Is it the discomfort with letting others down? Is it a desire to push the limits of life and stretch oneself thin?

To be honest, I am not all that interested in deducing whether my childhood scared me into saying "yes" or if I have a Superman complex or major *FOMO*. In this case, far more motivating than knowing the cause of this problem is to understand all its adverse effects.

As I have come to learn, to win at saying "yes" to all the things—even the ones that don't matter—is to possibly fail the people and things that matter most.

When I fail to say no, I wind up taking on responsibility for things that aren't my responsibility. Resultingly, I give a percentage of myself to things that don't require my attention at the expense of things that do — my actual jobs, my family, my health and well-being, just to name a few.

As a public speaker, I feel this all the time. Imagine it is a Monday afternoon and I am excited to begin writing a keynote that I have coming up on Friday. Low and behold, a colleague calls with a favor: "Trey, our speaker for an event on Thursday night bailed and we are all hoping you can save the day and give the talk."

Of course, the new commitment that I have taken on occurs the night before the event that I was actually looking forward to. After saying "yes" to this new responsibility, it becomes apparent that the topic they need me to speak on is somewhat familiar but will still require lots of prep time on my part.

Naturally, I agreed to "save the day" for my colleagues, but at what expense? Well, due to stretching it too thin, this hero without any cape gives a great but not excellent keynote on Friday (the one that I was excited about). So, that is a bummer, but it gets even more complicated.

You see, in addition to saying yes too often, I—like many of you—hate failing at anything. So, I choose to crank the midnight oil to make sure that both talks go as best as possible. I bring work with me to the park after school, so that I am technically spending time with my family but typing away while they kick the soccer ball. I also opt to stay up later than I should in order to get remaining work done while my family sleeps.

Do the math. There is only one Trey, yet I had to divide myself in order to save the day for a problem that wasn't mine. And now at least two things—the talk that I was excited about and time with my family—suffer so that I can play superman and save the day for a colleague in a jam.

Once every while, this would be no big deal. But what happens if saying yes to anything and everyone becomes the norm?

How many preferred projects, trips to the park with the family, and nights of sleep should be compromised so that I can say "yes" to a whole bunch of other problems that aren't mine to solve?

Learn from my mistakes. When a responsibility stares you in the face, ask first if it is really your problem to solve. If it is, own it and crush it!

If it is not your responsibility, but taking on the problem excites you, consider the cost and make a wise choice about whether, and to what extent, to get involved.

If it is not your responsibility, and you know in your gut that you want nothing to do with it, smile, decline the invitation to participate, and keep walking.

Build that muscle of knowing when and how to say no. The consequence of not doing so is to establish the horrible habit of taking on responsibilities that are not yours and that you wish did not monopolize your time. Like the courage to say yes, the courage to say no is a vital skill—not just in evading behaviors you know to be harmful, but also in protecting your time.

Our most precious gift

Time may be our most precious gift. How we choose to invest our time says a great deal about who we are and what we value. I urge my family, friends, colleagues, students, and all to love what you do. And do lots of what you love.

Many people around you chase breaks and retirement. Then they retire, talk about how bored they are, and complain that no one visits them. All that time wasted dreaming of easy street just to get there. And for what?! To experience atrophy and find yourself bored. That sounds awful! I'd rather work hard at the work worth doing and develop the courage to say yes (and no), to make the most of our most precious gift—time.

CRUCIAL
CONVERSATIONS

What about you—when you check yourself in the mirror, what do you find staring back at you saying, "Just do it!"?

What do you do with that inner-wisdom? How do you keep track of it? Who holds you accountable for actually doing anything with it?

Reflect on a time that you celebrated/regretted having/lacking the courage to say yes/no.

What in your life right now do you need to be saying "yes" to? And, conversely, who or what in your life right now do you need the courage to say no to?

How do you think about time? Have you come to discover it as a most precious gift? How does your view of time shape the way you spend it?

......
Want to share this conversation with Trey, or perhaps even see your thoughts in a future version of this book?

Go to treyguinn.com/adulting and share!

IN CONCLUSION,
AND ONWARD!

While this book is imperfect and incomplete, I conclude here comforted knowing that I have written with love, and made a good-faith, heartfelt attempt at sharing some trails and tales from Adulting Mountain. Even more, I hope to have inspired you to have more crucial conversations about who you are becoming. In these parting words, I offer an additional invitation to think deeply about the qualities and characteristics that you wish to be true of you.

My life has been made better by prayers boldly prayed for those things that I wish to be truer for my life. I regularly pray for increases of wisdom, courage, a heart that loves better, and much more. I invite you to name and claim those things you wish to be truer of life.

But do so fully aware that the answer will not come like fairy dust falling from the heavens. Instead, as it has been in my life, it may come to you in the gift of time and space to work-out those muscles. Asking for qualities like courage or patience are great examples. The next morning, you may not wake immediately possessing those qualities, but you may be presented with scenarios that require you to behave courageously or act with more patience.

Think of it like when you want money and someone says, "great, get a job." Similarly, when you want particular muscles to grow or character traits to ooze from you, it's great to name and claim it, BUT then be prepared to do the exercise necessary to grow it.

I pray that you have the boldness to name and claim the qualities and characteristics that you wish to be truer of you, the kinds of qualities that you know will serve you well on your hike through Adulting Mountain. And I also pray that you have the strength and stamina to chase after those things when you find them. I hope you will do the same for me. Let's not be like the person who looked in the mirror and saw what needed to be done, but then walked away. Instead, let's lace our boots and hike onward into richer adventures in adulting.

NOTES

1. Drake. "The Motto." Recorded 2011. Young Money. Cash Money. Republic, digital download.

2. Cyrus, Miley. "The Climb." Recorded 2009. Hollywood. CD single, digital download.

3. Metts, Sandra and Grohskopf, Erica. "Impression Management." In Handbook of Communication and Social Interaction Skills, edited by John O. Greene and Brant R. Burleson. Lawrence Erlbaum Associates, Inc., 2003. 357-402.

4. King Jr., Martin L. "The Purpose of Education." Maroon Tiger (Atlanta, GA), Feb. 1947.

5. Brooks, David. Road to Character. New York: Random House, 2016.

6. Matthews, David. "The Best of What's Around." Recorded 1994-2006. RCA. Bama Rags. Album.

7. Rowling, J.K. Harry Potter and the Chamber of Secrets. United Kingdom: Bloomsbury, 1998.

8. Guinn, Trey. "Friendship Work." Sage Journals 20, no. 6 (2016): 23-26.

9. Beatles. "All You Need Is Love." Recorded 1967. Parlophone. Capitol.

10. Sternberg, Robert. "Duplex Theory of Love: Triangular Theory of Love and Theory of Love as a Story." http://www.robertjsternberg.com/love

11. Parker Palmer, Let Your Life Speak: Listening for the Voice of Vocation. (New York: John Wiley & Sons, Inc. 2000).

12. Mineo, Liz. "Good genes are nice, but joy is better." Harvard Gazette. April 11, 2017. https://news.harvard.edu/gazette/story/2017/04/over-nearly-80-years-harvard-study-has-been-showing-how-to-live-a-healthy-and-happy-life.

ABOUT THE AUTHOR

Dr. Trey Guinn and his family reside in Texas. A university professor and department chair, Guinn is also an active author, actor, speaker, executive coach and consultant to clients globally. A key focus of his work is on human development, communication effectiveness and personal relationships. Friends say that the secret to his positivity and success is an attitude of gratitude, abiding faith, love for others, in addition to lots of running and coffee!

Trey can be reached at: treyguinn.com/adulting

Made in the USA
Coppell, TX
23 April 2021

54258703R10100